PUBLICATIONS OF THE DEPARTMENT OF ROMANCE LANGUAGES
UNIVERSITY OF NORTH CAROLINA

General Editor: ALDO SCAGLIONE

Editorial Board: JUAN BAUTISTA AVALLE-ARCE, PABLO GIL CASADO, FRED M. CLARK, GEORGE BERNARD DANIEL, JANET W. DÍAZ, ALVA V. EBERSOLE, AUGUSTIN MAISSEN, EDWARD D. MONTGOMERY, FREDERICK W. VOGLE

NORTH CAROLINA STUDIES IN THE
ROMANCE LANGUAGES AND LITERATURES

ESSAYS; TEXTS, TEXTUAL STUDIES AND TRANSLATIONS; SYMPOSIA

Founder: URBAN TIGNER HOLMES

Editor: JUAN BAUTISTA AVALLE-ARCE
Associate Editor: FREDERICK W. VOGLER

Other publications of the Department: *Estudios de Hispanófila, Hispanófila, Romance Notes, Studia Raeto-Romanica*

Distributed by:

INTERNATIONAL SCHOLARLY BOOK SERVICE, INC.
P. O. BOX 4347
Portland, Oregon   97208
U. S. A.

NORTH CAROLINA STUDIES IN THE
ROMANCE LANGUAGES AND LITERATURES
Number 136

ARTUS DÉSIRÉ
PRIEST AND PAMPHLETEER
OF THE SIXTEENTH CENTURY

ARTUS DÉSIRÉ
PRIEST AND PAMPHLETEER
OF THE SIXTEENTH CENTURY

BY

FRANK S. GIESE

CHAPEL HILL

NORTH CAROLINA STUDIES IN THE ROMANCE
LANGUAGES AND LITERATURES
U.N.C. DEPARTMENT OF ROMANCE LANGUAGES

1973

Library of Congress Cataloging in Publication Data

Giese, Frank S.
  Artus Désiré: priest and pamphleteer of the sixteenth century.
  (North Carolina studies in the Romance languages and literatures, no. 136).

  Bibliography: p. 15-17.

  1. Désiré, Artus. 2. Désiré, Artus — Bibliography. I. Title: Priest and pamphleteer of the sixteenth century. II. Series.
BX4705.D439G53   282' .092'4 [B]   73-14987

ISBN: 978-0-8078-9136-0

DEPÓSITO LEGAL: V. 4.474 - 1973

ARTES GRÁFICAS SOLER, S. A. — JÁVEA, 28 — VALENCIA (8) — 1973

TABLE OF CONTENTS

	Pages
PREFACE	9
BIBLIOGRAPHY of sources containing information on Artus Désiré and on his times; and on works by, or attributed to, him	15
CHAPTER I. LIFE OF ARTUS DÉSIRÉ	19
— II. BIBLIOGRAPHY OF EDITIONS OF DÉSIRÉ'S WORKS	36
— III. ANALYSIS OF THE WORKS OF DÉSIRÉ — INTRODUCTION	74
1. *Theological polemics*	
Miroer-Deffensoire (II)	77
Combatz (III)	86
Disputes de Guillot (XVI)	92
Articles (XV)	98
Grand chemin (XIX)	99
Desespoir testamentaire (VIII)	100
2. *Polemics dealing with Geneva*	
Passevent parisien (X)	102
Grandes chroniques (XIV)	109
3. *Hymnes, and polemics against Marot*	
Hymnes ecclésiastiques (VI)	116
Contrepoison (XVII)	120
4. *Miscellaneous pamphlets*	
Description philosophale (IX)	131
Regretz... Francois Picart (XII)	133
5. *Social commentaries*	
Loyauté des taverniers (IV)	135
Grands jours (V)	139
Instruction chrestienne (VII)	142

Origine et source (XXI)	145
Desorde et scandale (XXII)	148
Singerie des Huguenots (XXIII)	150
Ravage et deluge (XXIV)	152
Retour de Guillot (XXIV)	156

CHAPTER IV. AN INÉDIT OF ARTUS DÉSIRÉ: *SECRET CONSEIL AU ROY* CHARLES IX. 1568 (XX) ... 161

CONCLUSION ... 184

PREFACE

Although the name of Artus Désiré, priest and pamphleteer of the 16th century in France, is well known to specialists in the polemical literature of that period, there has been no comprehensive study of his career. By bringing together as much information as possible about the man and his works, the present work is intended to fill this gap. It is not the purpose of this study to prove any particular thesis, but it is felt that any new information on the religious wars and their origin is of importance.

Throughout the 18th and early 19th centuries he was known to bibliophiles as the ungifted author of a long list of oddly titled volumes, all extremely rare. Several of these were the subject of articles in the *Bulletin du Bibliophile;* and Brunet's *Manuel du libraire et de l'amateur de livres* of 1861, and its *Supplément,* listed over sixty editions of close to twenty separate works. Meanwhile, as an intransigent foe of the French protestants, Désiré figured several times in the *Bulletin de la Société de l'histoire du Protestantisme français.*

In modern times some material relative to his career is to be found in:

1. Charles Lenient, in a few pages in his study of 16th century satire;
2. Alfred Cartier, in an article dealing with a minor work of Désiré, the *Grandes chroniques et annales;*
3. Helen Shaw, who discussed Désiré briefly for the role he was made to play in the *Comédie du pape malade,* attributed to Conrad Badius;

4. A Cioranesco, who made a new listing of his works in his bibliography of the 16th century;
5. C. A. Mayer, who investigated his role as an orthodox critic of Marot's translations of the psalms.

Artus Désiré, whose career extended from 1545 to at least 1578, was the author of more than twenty theological treatises and anti-Protestant pamphlets, most of them in rhyme, in over one hundred editions. Despite his literary shortcomings, he was a formidable polemicist; and judging from the bulk alone of his published works, his voice must have carried some weight in his own time.

Without talent, with a strictly orthodox education and no interest in classical antiquity, with a profound distrust of intellectual curiosity and no understanding whatever of the reformation, Artus Désiré lived his life untouched by any aspect of the Renaissance.

What interest he has today lies in his activity as a propagandist for the Catholic cause in France. At a moment when most of the resistance to the new ideas was still centered in the Sorbonne and in official quarters, and published in Latin when published at all, Désiré was one of the first to carry the fight for religious conformity and intolerance before the public, and in a language it could understand. His blind intolerance, his willful slander, and the violence of his proposals to curb the heretics, made him a fitting link between Noel Béda and the League. Further, the low quality of his arguments helps to explain the formation of that segment of public opinion which was finally roused to approve the extermination of the dissidents.

Artus Désiré stands outside the usually-accepted literary pale: there is no mention of his name in Lanson's bibliography, for example. Still his works have some slight literary pretension; and they throw enough light on the temper of the times to merit this exhumation, if not a rehabilitation of their author's name.

The form of this work has been determined by the nature of the materials available. A general bibliography of the sources of information on Artus Désiré has been placed first; subsequent references to these sources will give only such details as are necessary to easy identification. After a brief biography (there are not many facts available on his life, and few of these are new), there is a bibliography of his works. This is fuller than any previous listing but is probably not complete. A longer section is then devoted to an analysis of his works, both major and minor, and his role in the important controversies in which he played a part. Finally I have appended the hitherto unpublished text of a poem of close to 600 lines, which he addressed to Charles IX in 1568, as a "Secret conseil."

Thanks are offered to all those who have assisted in the preparation of this work, especially to the personnel of the librairies of Paris: Nationale, Arsenal, Mazarine, Sainte-Geneviève, and Bibliothèque du Protestantisme; also a special word of gratitude to M. A. Cioranesco, for his kindness in pointing out to me certain bibliographical sources not generally available.

GENERAL BIBLIOGRAPHY

Listing works containing information
on the life and works of

ARTUS DÉSIRÉ

BIBLIOGRAPHY OF SOURCES CONTAINING INFORMATION ON
ARTUS DÉSIRÉ AND ON HIS TIMES; AND ON WORKS BY,
OR ATTRIBUTED TO, HIM

Armstrong, Elizabeth, *Robert Estienne, Royal Printer. An Historical Study of the Elder Stephanus.* Cambridge, Cambridge University Press, 1954.
Arrests et procès verbaulx d'execution d'iceux, contre Jean Tanquerel, Désiré, François Bossère et autres. Paris, 1580. 36 pp. Pages 19-20.
Badius, Conrad, *La Comédie du pape malade.* Text contained in Shaw, Helen. *Conrad Badius and the Comédie du pape malade.* Philadelphia, 1934.
Baird, Henry M., *History of the rise of the Huguenots of France.* N.Y. Chas. Scribner's Sons, 1879. 2 vol.
Baudrier, *Bibliographie lyonnaise: Recherches sur les imprimeurs, libraires, et fondeurs de lettres de Lyon au XVIe siècle.* Paris, (réimpression) F. de Nobele, 1964.
Berthoud, G. et al, *Aspects de la propagande religieuse.* (Travaux d'Humanisme et Renaissance, XXVIII). Geneva, Droz, 1957.
Bèze, Th. de, *Le Passavant de Theodore de Beze.* Ed. Lizieux, Paris, 1875.
——, *Vie de Calvin.* Publiée et annotée par Alfred Franklin. Nouv. éd. Paris, 1869.
Briquet, Appolin, Notice on *Le grand chemin céleste,* in *Bulletin du Bibliophile,* 1855, pp. 503-4.
Brunet, Jacques-Charles, *Manuel du libraire et de l'amateur de livres.* 5th edition. Paris, Firmin Didot, 1861. 5 vol. II, col. 627-631.
——, Article: "Désiré, Artus," in Nouvelle bibliographie générale, XIII, 831.
Brunet, G. and Deschamps, *Supplément au Manuel du libraire.* Paris, no date. col. 387-9.
Bulletin du Bibliophile. Paris, 1834 to present. Scattered articles.
Bulletin de la Société de l'histoire du Protestantisme français. Paris, 1852 to present. Scattered articles.
Calvin, Jean, *Œuvres françoises de Jean Calvin.* Ed. Paul Lacroix, Paris, Charles Gosselin, 1842.
Cartier, Alfred, Article: "Les Genevois en 1558 d'apres un libelle contemporain. Les grandes Chroniques et Annales de Passepartout par A. Désiré," in *Mémoires et documents publiés par la Société d'histoire et d'archéologie de Genève.* No. 5, 1893-1901, pp. 163-202.

Catherine de Médicis, *Lettres de Catherine de Médicis, publiées par M. le Comte Hector de la Ferrière.* Tome premier, Vols. I and II. Tome second, 1563-1566. Paris, Imprimerie Nationale 1880.

Chaix, Paul, *Recherches sur l'Imprimerie à Genève de 1550 à 1564 Etude bibliographique, économique et littéraire.* Geneva, Droz, 1954.

Charbonnier, F., *La poésie française et les guerres de religion.* Thèse. Grenoble, Paris, Bureau de la Revue des œuvres nouvelles, 1919. Scattered references.

Cioranesco, A., *Bibliographie de la littérature française du XVIe siècle.* Paris, Klincksieck, 1959, pp. 240-241.

Dictionnaire de biographie française publié sous la direction de Roman d'Amat. Paris, 1965.

Dictionnaire des lettres françaises, XVIe siècle. Article: "Désiré, Artus."

Doumergue, Emile, *Iconographie calvinienne.* Lausanne, G. Bridel, 1909.

Du Roure, Marquis, *Analectabiblion, ou Extraits critiques de divers livres rares, oubliés ou peu connus.* Paris, 1836-7. 2 vol. I, pp. 429-33.

Du Verdier, A., *Les Bibliothèques françoises de La Croix du Maine et de Du Verdier.* Paris, 1772. 5 vol. I, 60; III, 99, 167-9.

Gachet d'Artigny, abbé A., *Nouveaux mémoires d'histoire, de critique et de littérature.* Paris, Debure l'aîné, 1749-56. 7 vol. II, 41-48.

Goujet, abbé Claude Pierre, *Bibliothèque françoise, ou Histoire de la Littérature françoise....* Paris, 1741-56. 18 vol. XIII, 129-41; XIV, 423-8.

Heist, William, *"Sermon Joyeux" and Polemic: Two Sixteenth-Century applications of the Legend of the Fifteen Signs.* (Studies in the Romance Languages and Literatures #72). Chapel Hill, North Carolina, University of North Carolina Press, 1968.

Histoire ecclésiastique. Ed. Reuss. Paris, Fischbacher, 1883-89. 3 vol. I, pp. 814-820 plus scattered references.

Klipffel, Henri, *Le Colloque de Poissy, étude sur la crise religieuse et politique en 1561....* Paris, Librairie Internationale, 1867.

———, *Quis fuerit in Gallia Factionum status circa annum 1561 et colloquium Possiaci habitum; Facultati litterarum Parisiensi Thesim proponebat.* MDCCCLXIII.

Kuttner, Stephan et al eds., *Traditio: Studies in Ancient and Medieval History, Thought and Religion.* Vol. XXII. New York, Fordham University Press, 1966.

Lachèvre, Frédéric, *Bibliographie des recueils collectifs de poésie du XVIe siècle.* Paris, 1922.

La Fosse, Jehan de, *Journal d'un curé ligueur sous les trois derniers Valois.* ed. Ed. de Barthélemy. Paris, 1886.

Lavisse, Ernest, *Histoire de France illustrée, depuis les origines jusqu'à la Révolution.* Tome VI. Première partie. *La Réforme et la ligue, L'Edit de Nantes (1559-1598)* par J. H. Mariéjol. Paris, Hachette, 1911.

Le Fevre, Jean, *Dictionnaire des rimes françoises. Premierement composé par Jean le Fevre Dijonnais, Chanoine de Langres et de Bar-sur-Aube; Et depuis augmenté, corrigé, et mis en bon ordre, par le Seigneur des Accords.* Paris, Jean Richer, 1587.

Lenient, Charles, *La satire en France, ou la littérature militante au XVIe siècle.* Paris, 1866. pp. 221-4.

Lenoir, Paulette, *La Poésie religieuse de Clément Marot.* Paris, Nizet, 1955.

Lonchamp, F. C., *Manuel du Bibliophile Français, 1470-1920*. Paris and Lausanne, Librairie de Bibliophiles, 1927. 2 vol. I, 195; II, 129.
Mayer, C. A., *La religion de Marot*. Geneva, Droz, 1960. pp. 85-91.
Niceron, père Jean-Pierre, *Mémoires pour servir à l'histoire des hommes illustres dans la république des lettres, avec un catalogue raisonné de leurs ouvrages*. Paris, Briasson, 1727-45. 43 vol. XXXV, 284 ff.
Pasquier, Etienne, *Lettres historiques pour les années 1556-1594 publiées et annotées par D. Thickett*. Geneva, Droz, 1966.
Picot, Emile, *Catalogue des livres composant la bibliothèque de feu M. le baron James de Rothschild*. Paris, Morgand, 1884-1920. 5 vol.
———, "Fichier d'E. Picot," BN Mss. Fr. Nouv. Acq. 23,217.
Rasse des Nœux, Manuscript collection, BN Mss. Fr. 22,560-22,565.
Sallengre, Albert-Henri de, *Mémoires de littérature*. La Haye, 1715-17. 2 vol. II, 110-112.
Satyres chrétiennes de la cuisine papale. Geneva, 1560.
Shaw, Helen, *Conrad Badius and the Comédie du pape malade*. Philadelphia, 1934.
Singulier antidote contre le poison des chansons d'Artus Désiré . . . . fait par J. D. D. C. No city. 1561.
de Thou, Jac. *Augusti Thuani Historiarum sui temporis*. Tomus secundus. London, Samuel Buckley, 1733. Liber XXVIII (1561), vol. xvii.
Varillas, le sieur, *Histoire de Charles IX*. Paris, Claude Barbin, 1686. 2 vol. I, 129-30.
Viollet-le-Duc, *Catalogue des livres composant la bibliothèque poétique de M. Viollet-le-Duc, avec des notes bibliographiques, biographiques et littéraires sur chacun des ouvrages catalogués*. Paris, Hachette, 1843. pp. 262-263.
Weiss, N., Review in *Bulletin de la Société de l'Histoire du Protestantisme Français*, vol. 49 (1900), p. 652, of Lacombe, Bernard de, "Les Débuts des guerres de religion, Orléans, 1559-1564."
Yates, Francis A., *The Valois Tapestries*. London, The Warburg Institute, University of London, 1959.

CHAPTER I

LIFE OF ARTUS DÉSIRÉ

I

Very little is known with certainty about the life of Artus Désiré. In the words of Niceron, he "n'est connu que par un grand nombre de mauvais ouvrages, qui ne sont recherchés des curieux qu'à cause de leur rareté, et que par une action qui méritait la corde." [1]

"On ignore de quel pays il étoit," continued the eminent 18th-century bibliophile, himself a Catholic clergyman, "et l'on ne sçait le temps ni de sa naissance, ni de sa mort." [2] Abbé Goujet, in an effort to complete the notice given by Niceron, supposed that "il étoit Normand, parce que dans son livre intitulé *Les Combats du fidele Papiste....*, on voit qu'il prend un intérêt particulier à la Normandie, et qu'il ne fait mention d'aucun autre pays." [3] This conjecture is supported by a reference in the *Passavant* of Théodore de Bèze to Artus Désiré and "ses admirables rimes de Normandie" ("in suis mirabilibus rithmis Normanniae"). [4]

Goujet made no attempt to guess the date of his birth; but he offered a clue to the time of his death: ".... dès 1568 il recommença à publier différens ouvrages à Paris, comme il avoit fait auparavant. Le dernier est de 1578. Il est probable qu'il vécut peu après cette année: dans son écrit intitulé, *Le Retour de*

---

[1] Niceron, *Mémoires*, XXXV, 284.
[2] Ibid.
[3] Goujet, *Bibliothèque françoise*, XIII, 129.
[4] Bèze, *Epistola.... Passavanti*, pp. 12-13.

Guillot le Porcher, qui est à la suite du *Ravage et Deluge des chevaux de louage,* imprimé en 1578, il se représente comme étant vieux et grison." [5] Brunet supported this supposition, noting that he had died "vers 1579, à ce qu'on suppose, car son dernier ouvrage est daté de 1578, et le trépas seul pouvoit arrêter sa verve d'écrivain." [6]

This date, however, is by no means certain. As late as 1587 Désiré's name appeared as author of two liminary poems in a *Dictionnaire des rimes françoises.* [7] He is undoubtedly also the author of a little work published in 1587 entitled *Les Quinze Signes Advenues es parties d'Occident.* Although he may have written these opuscules much earlier, there is no evidence that he did so.

There is equal uncertainty about the date of his birth. Brunet offered 1500; [8] the *Dictionnaire des lettres* [9] and Cioranesco [10] both give 1510 as a rough guess. It is difficult to imagine that he waited until very late in life before entering a career which he then

---

[5] Goujet, loc. cit.

[6] Brunet, J. C., article: "Désiré, Artus," in *Nouv. biog. gén.,* XIII, 831.

[7] Jean le Fevre, *Dictionnaire des rimes françoises.* Paris, 1587. It may be of interest to include here the text of the two slight contributions by Artus Désiré.

    I.   Quand un livre est fait en Latin
           Grec, Turcq ou tel parler sauvage,
           Il advient que soir et matin
           On le met en autre langage.
           Mais ce volume en son totage
           Reçoit si grand' proprieté
           Qu'en sa forme et propre langage
           Il ne peut estre translaté.

    II.   Translateurs quittez la science
           Qu'avez de livres translater
           Car ce livre est sans patience
           Qu'on le puisse hors France porter.
           Et si vous cuidez attenter
           Le mettre en Grec, Suabe, ou Frison,
           Vous serez veu trop caqueter
           Par escrit sans rime et raison

[8] Brunet, loc. cit.

[9] *Dictionnaire des lettres françaises.* Vol. I (16th century). Article: "Désiré, Artus."

[10] Cioranesco, A., *Bibliographie de la littérature française au XVIe siècle,* pp. 240-41.

pursued with such enthusiasm; but lacking documentàry evidence, any date offered must remain a supposition.

According to Niceron again, "il est sûr seulement qu'il étoit prêtre." [11] Not only is this implicit in almost everything he wrote; but he stated it as a fact at least twice: in a *requête* addressed to Charles IX in 1561,[12] and in a *Secret conseil* to the same monarch in 1568.[13]

From 1545 onward, the flow of pamphlets from his pen continued with no real interruption until it finally dwindled about 1586.[14] There were over one hundred editions of his various works; these were more than twenty in number, distributed among three distinct periods of his career; a first group from 1545 to 1553; a new burst of activity from 1558 to 1561; and a final series of opuscules between 1568 and 1578. But reeditions continued to appear with some regularity throughout this entire period and until about 1586, after which date they virtually ceased. During the regency of Marie de Médicis, however, several of the Désiré pamphlets were again published.

II

During the decade of the 1560's, Artus Désiré made a series of at least three interventions in the political affairs of France. We cannot hope to explain these efforts to influence policy without first examining the basis and direction of that policy.

Following the death of her husband Henri II in 1559, Catherine de Médicis, as regent for her sons, assumed direct control of the affairs of state. During the 1560's, beset on all sides by forces desirous of sharing or even usurping the royal power, she adopted a flexible policy, continually facing the greatest threat of the moment by allying herself with lesser threats. As a result her alliances were constantly shifting, and her policy might appear excessively vacillating were it not for the fact that she never ceased

---

[11] Niceron, loc. cit.
[12] *Hist. ecclés.*, I, 819.
[13] See chap. IV of this work for text of *Secret Conseil*.
[14] See next chap. of this work for list of his works and editions.

to pursue the interests of the royal family which were to her identical with those of the country.

One of Catherine's major concerns was to prevent the controversy between Huguenots and Catholics from permanently tearing the country apart. Catherine's personal adherence to at least a formal catholicism was never seriously in doubt. However, her first concern was the integrity of the royal power; and the interplay of forces capable of undermining that power was exceedingly complex. There was not one single catholic faction, there were a variety of conflicting interests pursued by a number of catholic leaders. The Guise family, most closely identified with a strict line on orthodox catholicism, had ambitions to lay hands on the royal power of France. The Parlement of Paris, perhaps equally orthodox, was likewise jealous of its civil prerogatives, sometimes at odds with the interest of the crown. Philip II of Spain was not only married to a daughter of Catherine, he also had interests in the Low Countries as well as a maritime rivalry with England. Catherine could always count on him when she needed a powerful ally in the catholic camp, but she could never be certain that his ambitions might not encompass more than a defense of the faith.

Then too, many French prelates, representatives of the most important families in France, owed their nomination to the king, and though staunchly catholic were Gallican in attitude and fearful of papal power.

On the other side, Huguenots too had their representatives in important families, principally the Châtillons and Bourbons, and it was not always certain at what point genuine religious fervor gave way to political ambitions. Just as the Catholics could rely on Philip of Spain, but at some ultimate risk to the integrity of France, the Huguenots could turn for support to Protestant Elizabeth of England, but not without furthering her ambitions to occupy certain cities on the French coast, notably Calais and Le Havre.

It was the precariousness of her position as defender of the interests of her sons, first Francois II, then Charles IX, against these varied threats to their power, which pushed Catherine into the series of shifting alliances which gave her reign the appearance of instability, and seemed to support the accusation that her defense of the catholic cause was something less than constant.

In these circumstances, it is not difficult to understand the political posture of Artus Désiré, nor to divine his political alliances. His own theological position was clear and uncompromising to the point of frustration. In a choice between gallicanism, with its strong taint of corruption in the distribution of benefices, and the papal authority, his allegiance was to the Pope. The party that most closely echoed his sympathies was the Parlement of Paris, it too *ultramontain* and orthodox in the extreme. And the foreign ally most likely to sympathize with this position was Philip of Spain. Seen from this standpoint, there is total consistency in Artus Désiré's interventions.

We are fairly well informed about only one episode of his career in this period, an action for which Niceron felt that he "méritoit la corde." Following the "tumulte d'Amboise," the bloody repression of 1560 which concluded a clumsy effort by Protestant leaders to kidnap the king, a certain détente was fostered in official circles towards those of the new religion. In fact both Catherine de Médicis and the new chancellor, Michel de l'Hôpital, were anxious to calm the passions aroused among Protestants and Catholics alike. It was to this end that a colloquy was arranged for September and October 1561 between theological leaders of both camps, at Poissy near Paris. Both the regent and her minister seem to have genuinely hoped that a compromise on important disputes of doctrine could be worked out which would put an end to the danger of continued civil strife. For several months, Protestants circulated freely in Paris and other cities, and Huguenot services were held and attended by members of the royal family, even at Fontainebleau.

The *Colloque de Poissy* failed to achieve its goal and was disbanded by mid-October. But the threat of a compromise which would give the heretics some legal standing in France was apparently great enough in 1561 to inspire some of the more intransigent in the Catholic party to solicit the active intervention of Philip II of Spain in the dispute. Possibly self-sppointed but probably the instrument of more important figures, Artus Désiré set out in early spring on a futile mission as messenger to Philip.

A full though highly partisan account of his adventure is to be found in the *Histoire ecclésiastique:*

Quelques-uns de Paris, en ces entrefaits, tant des docteurs de Sorbonne que d'autres des plus grands zelateurs de la religion Romaine, desesperans de leurs affaires, s'oublierent tant que d'entreprendre de solliciter le *Roy d'Espagne* de se vouloir mesler de l'estat du royaume de France à bon escient. Et pour le comble de leur audace et follie, choisirent pour leur messager un certain prestre rimailleur, des plus impertinens hommes du monde, nommé *Artus Désiré*. Mais outre qu'il n'est vraysemblable que le Roy d'Espagne eust voulu prester l'aureille à une telle entreprise, la providence de Dieu y besongna, ayant esté descouvert ce dessein par un certain peintre de la *Royne mere*, nommé *Nicolas*, lequel en ayant donné l'advertissement à Orléans, où il savoit que ce messager avoit son adresse chés le Curé de Sainct Paterne, homme de mesme humeur que luy, l'affaire fut si bien conduite, qu'*Artus* s'estant mis sus l'eau pour descendre jusques à Tours ou plus loin, fut surpris avec son paquet par le Prevost des Mareschaux d'Orléans, au commencement du mois de Mars. Et pource que choses de si grande conséquence se trouverent en ce paquet, il fut advisé qu'on meneroit le prisonnier au Roy, ce qui fut fait. [15]

How Désiré happened to be seized is explained facetiously in the *Comédie du Pape malade,* in which Désiré accuses his accomplice, Jacques Guéset, curé de Saint Paterne, of responsibility for his seizure, because of his personal vanity:

> Et que le grand diable y ait part
> Si j'eusse avancé mon départ
> Ceci ne fust point advenu.
> Saint Eustace m'a retenu,
> Ce beau curé de triqueniques
> S'amusant apres ces guenippes...
> ... ...
> Et toy, notable Paternier,
> N'es-tu pas un grand lanternier
> De m'avoir ainsi retenu
> Et tousjours en abboy tenu
> Tant que tes bottes fussent prestes,
> Et ton chaperon de grandes festes... [16]

---

[15] *Hist. ecclés.*, I, 813. This account of events is confirmed by both de Thou and Varillas, among others, as well as in *Singulier Antidote*.

[16] Badius, C., *La Comédie du pape malade*, ed. H. Shaw, lines 1179 ff.

The *Histoire ecclésiastique* quoted in full the request to Philip for intervention, "escrit en grande feuille de vellin, en letre fort menue, que j'ay bien voulu inserer de mot à mot, non pas que tels badinages valent le publier, mais afin que la postérité cognoisse et deteste aussi bien l'insuffisance que la mauvaistié de tels esprits:

> Cher Sire, Roy tres-catholique, Prince treschrestien, esleu par la grace de Dieu, des plus sapiens, supreme et souverain Seigneur de tout le monde, pour le regime, gouvernement, et defense de sa republique Chrestienne, treshumble salut. Le zele grand, o Sire, de la maison de Dieu, a tellement devoré consumé et mangé en nous la timidité, crainte et peur de nos personnes, que nous sommes totalement asseurés de vostre treschrestien vouloir et desir de corriger, et punir, vaincre et debeller tous les profuges et bannis de la saincte societé et congregation des vrays fideles et catholiques. A la requeste desquels, et en special de la part de tous vos treshumbles et tresobeissans clergé, bourgeois, marchans et menu peuple de la ville, cité et université de Paris, preservés et gardés par grace speciale de Dieu jusques aujourdhuy, de la veneneuse et mortifere poison Lutherienne; nous venons pardevant vostre tresnoble et tressacrée majesté vous supplier et requerir et prier treshumblement qu'il vous plaise, de vostre benigne grace et clemence acoustumée tousjours augmenter, accroistre, et persister au bon vouloir et zele grand que nostre Seigneur vous a donné pour soustenir, ayder et defendre sa saincte et fructueuse religion Chrestienne... donner courage, confort et ayde de vostre parole audit populaire Chrestien envers tous Magistrats et gouverneurs de France, qui pour le jourdhuy donnent telle faveur, puissance et authorité aux ennemis de nostre foy Catholique, que chacun estime devoir advenir de brief un si grand trouble, sedition, et preparation de mort sanguinolente entre les Chrestiens, si par la creation du monde ne fut venue telle calamité, misere, pauvreté, et tribulation qu'on verra estre entre le pere et le fils, et Royaume contre Royaume.... Et pource que nous voyons ledit royaume en peril, et danger d'estre du tout subverti et perdu, et encores, ce qui est beaucoup à craindre, que nostre jeune Roy treschrestien sous bas aage, n'en soit au temps advenir instruit et contaminé, nous sommes venus vous advertir et informer de toutes ces choses, comme le plus prochain du sang et auquel en appartient la

> cognoissance et reformation, et non à l'autre....; pour auxquelles choses obvier et remedier, supplions derechef treshumblement vostre tressacrée majesté en la vertu de Dieu et amour de Chrestienté, prester la main à son Eglise gallicane, et advertir si bien les magistrats et gouverneurs dudit royaume de France, que vos admonitions, remonstrances et advertissements leur servent d'une verge de correction, crainte et amendement, pour les garder et empescher de ne mettre à execution leur deliberation et entreprise, telle que le bruit est, et qu'on estime devoir avenir de bref, si de vostre grace et misericorde n'y est donné par vous empeschement.... [17]

"Chacun peut voir," continued the author, "par la lecture de ce que dessus, ce que meritoit non seulement ce malheureux, mais aussi ceux qui l'avoient mis en besongne." [18] But, in the words of Niceron now, "la crainte du supplice qu'il méritoit, lui fit adresser deux requêtes, l'une au Roi, et l'autre à la Reine Mère, pour demander comme une grace, qu'on eut pitié de lui, et qu'on se contentât de le condamner à une prison perpétuelle ou aux Galères pour le reste de sa vie, afin qu'il pût faire pénitence." [19]

> *Requeste au Roy:* Supplie treshumblement *Artus Désiré*, povre prestre, le plus dolent, miserable et malheureux pecheur envers vos personnes et autres princes et grands seigneurs par luy offensés, que le feu, le ciel et la terre demandent vengeance de ses crimes de leze majesté à l'encontre de luy. Toutefois sachant bien et cognoissant que le propre usage des princes est d'estre misericordieux envers leurs povres sujets, suivant le commendement de nostre Seigneur, se confiant du tout en leur clemence et bonté, vous supplie tous de tout son cœur, force et puissance, luy remettre la vie, et par la charité et bonté qu'avès en Dieu et vostredit prochain, luy ordonner pour ses demerites prison perpetuelle seulement, ou les galeres, pour et afin qu'il ayt moyen de faire penitence, et de ne l'envoyer devant le jugement de Dieu, lequel il craint

---

[17] *Hist. ecclés.*, I, 814-819. This document, filling between 5 and 6 large pages in the Reuss edition, is not quoted in full here; enough is given, however, to demonstrate its intention, and also its style, which closely resembles that of Désiré's other prose works.

[18] Ibid.

[19] Niceron, loc. cit.

sans comparaison plus que la mort corporelle. Et ce faisans, à tousjours et à jamais priera pour vostre santé et prosperité, requerant derechef misericorde à vous tous, messeigneurs, en ce temps idoine aux pauvres penitens, misericorde, misericorde, misericorde. [20]

Requeste à la Royne mère: A Madame la Regente: Artus Desiré. O noble dame misericordieuse, pour la charité et amour de feu treschrestien Roy Henry vostre espoux, que Dieu absolve, lequel m'envoya faire une neufvieme à Nostre dame de Lorette, plaise vous me remettre la vie et estre mon intercedente envers monsieur le Roy de Navarre, et messieurs le Cardinal de Lorraine et de Chastillon, me pardonner et m'ordonner prison, ou gallere perpetuelle pour le reste de mes ans, et pour prier perpetuellement pour le Roy, pour vous et pour tous mes seigneurs, car je crains grandement le jugement de Dieu, plus que mort corporelle. [20]

When compared with his constant appeals to each king in turn to exterminate the heretics for the greater glory of God, his request to Charles IX on his own behalf, on the grounds that "le propre usage des princes est d'estre misericordieux envers leurs povres sujets, suivant le commandement de nostre Seigneur" strikes an incongruous note.

"Le Parlement," continued Niceron, "le traita plus favorablement qu'il n'avoit pû l'espérer." [21] He received, in fact, the surprisingly mild sentence of "amende honorable" and five years' seclusion in the Chartreux monastery near Paris. The exact terms of the sentence were:

Dict a esté, que ladite Cour a condamné et condamne ledit Désiré, pour raison des cas mentionnez audit proces, à faire amende honorable au parquet de ladite Cour a jour de plaidoyrie; et pour ce faire y estre mené, estant teste et pieds nuds, tenant en ses mains une torche de cire ardente du poix de deux livres, et illec estant à genoux dire et declarer, Que temmerairement, malicieusement, et comme mal-advisé, il a escrit et dressé la requeste maintenue au proces, et essayé la porter où bon luy auroit

---

[20] *Hist. ecclés.*, I, 819.
[21] Niceron, loc. cit.

semblé, dont il se repent, et en requiert mercy et pardon à Dieu, au Roy, et à justice. Et sera ladite requeste lacerée en sa presence, et ce fait estre mené et conduit au monastere et religion des Chartreux lez ceste ville de Paris, pour faire penitence le temps et espace de cinq ans. Prononceé et executé quant à ladite amende honorable, et laceration de ladite requeste, le lundi 14 jour de Juillet l'an 1561. Ainsi signé, Malon. Nota qu'il avoit esté ordonné que ledit Désiré feroit pareille amende honorable sur la Table de marbre, et sur le perron des grans degrez du Palais, et que ladite peine pour aucunes considerations fut mitigée." [22]

Who was behind this abortive plot, and what was the extent of Désiré's responsibility? It is hard to be sure. Désiré himself, in his *requête* to Philip, claimed to speak for the clergy and other estates of Paris. This is vague, and he does not appear to have implicated anyone else in the course of his trial. Further, the *requête* itself bears the unmistakable stamp of his own style.

His real allies in this project, and quite possibly its instigators, are probably to be found in the Parlement of Paris, but there is no documentary proof of this. The *Histoire ecclésiastique* mentions merely the initiative of "quelques-uns de Paris." Varillas saw in the event a sign that the League was already in process of formation. [23] This is largely a technical question, since the elements that later were to form the League were already active, and they included many from the Parlement. Klipffel offers no substantiation for his theory that Cardinal de Lorraine was behind the adventure, but this is certainly a possibility. [24]

Further evidence that Désiré's backers included the Parlement is to be found in the surprisingly mild sentence he received, and the ease with which he escaped serving it. At the same time that she was arranging the *Colloque de Poissy* between doctrinal spokesmen for both Catholics and Protestants, Catherine herself was negotiating with the king of Spain to forestall his intervention in the affairs of France. [25]

---

[22] *Arrest et proces verbaulx*, etc. . . . *contre Artus Désiré*, etc. pp. 19-20.
[23] Varillas, *Hist. de Ch. IX*, II, 129.
[24] Klipffel, *Le Colloque de Poissy*, p. 170.
[25] *Hist. ecclés.*, I, 120. "Par une lettre de Catherine de Médicis à l'évèque de Limoges, du 16 avril 1561, elle annonce elle-même qu'elle a consenti à ce

In those circumstances, Désiré's efforts to undermine the royal policy would seem all the more serious, and his light sentence and subsequent escape from confinement the more surprising, if he did not enjoy some important protection, which certainly did not come from the court.

The *Histoire ecclésiastique* attributes his light sentence specifically to the influence of friends in the Parlement;[26] Varillas to persons higher than the Parlement, which in his opinion feared what a thorough investigation might reveal.[27]

In any case, according to the *Histoire ecclésiastique* "il fut confiné au Couvent des Chartreux, dont toutefois il sortit, peu après, et n'en a on oui parler depuis."[28] The *Journal* of Jehan de la Fosse adds that "il y fut quatre moys.... Depuis il ne se cacha pas et se promenoit à Paris."[29] The brevity of the incarceration is confirmed by two lines in the *Comédie du pape malade,* in which Désiré is represented as complaining to his colleague, the curé of Saint Paterne:

> Tu m'as fait faire une gésine
> De sept mois dedans un croton...[30]

The four months mentioned by Jehan de la Fosse refer to his imprisonment after sentencing. Adding these to the four months in custody while awaiting trial, we reach a total imprisonment of slightly more than seven months. It may be significant that this would place the date of his liberation sometime in November 1561, at a time when, royal efforts at reconciliation having failed,

---

que plusieurs seigneurs de la cour écrivissent en Espagne pour temoigner de l'état de la religion en France, afin qu'on voie bien qu'elle ne veut nullement changer de foi, comme le publient ses ennemis. Elle désire que le Roy Catholique voie cette lettre. Voy, un catalogue de Techener, Paris, 1841, p. 261." — Note by editors.

[26] *Hist. ecclés.,* I, 820.
[27] Varillas, loc. cit.
[28] *Hist. ecclés.,* I, 120.
[29] Jehan de la Fosse, *Journal d'un cure ligueur sous les trois derniers Valois,* p. 43 ("juillet 1561"). Although inserted as of July 1561, this information must have been added later, since this was the month in which sentence was imposed. His escape would thus have occurred about the month of November.
[30] Badius, *La Comédie du pape malade,* lines 1196-7.

Désiré could no longer endanger the success of the Colloque de Poissy.

That Désiré used his freedom to continue to make himself objectionable to the royal authority is clear. During the summer of 1564, Catherine was endeavoring to have the Parlement of Paris register an edict of pacification whose terms included the disarming of the population of Paris. "L'ordre du désarment avait provoqué dans tout Paris une vive agitation. En pleine chaire, un moine, Artus Désiré, avait invité le peuple à ne pas céder et à garder ses armes. Le 23 août, Lansac vint se plaindre au Parlement du scandale de pareils propos et du retard apporte à l'enregistrement de l'Edit. Le Président de Thou affirma que une prise de Corps avait été décrétée contre Artus Désiré et que le retard ne tenait qu'à la maladie du rapporteur." [31] In fact, an edict of Charles IX, dated July 19, 1564, stated that "Sa Majesté entend que Artus Désiré soit banny du royaume, et s'il y retourne, qu'il soit bien et vivement chastié." [32]

Nothing is known of his whereabouts for the next four years. However, despite the interdiction, Désiré in 1568 returned to his campaign against the Huguenots and their sympathizers, with a "Secret Conseil" to the king urging the extermination of all religious dissidents. [33] Here again a glance at the history of these years may help to relate the few known facts of Désiré's career to the events of the time.

The second of the long series of religious wars broke out in 1567 and the Protestants were to suffer several severe defeats before the peace of Longjumeau was achieved in 1568. But despite the open hostilities of this period, the political alignments within the nation were such that powerful voices sympathetic to the Huguenot cause, or at least anxious for an end to the bloodshed, continued to be heard at court. That the dissidents were far from isolated at this time is indicated by the facts that, as soon as peace had again returned in 1570, the marriage of Henri de Navarre, military chief of the Protestants, was arranged with Marguerite de Valois, sister of the king; and that Colligny, chief

---

[31] *Lettres de Catherine de Médicis*, II, Introd. p. xxiv.
[32] *Mémoires de Condé*, éd. de 1743. Vol. 44 (quoted by Picot, "Fichier.")
[33] See Chap. II, XX, 101, and chap. IV, "An inédit of Artus Désiré.")

spokesman for the Huguenots at the court, became a respected personal adviser to Charles IX.

No doubt with the dual purpose of regaining his own right to be heard in France and of putting an end to a situation in which the party which to him stood for heresy, treason and open rebellion continued to maintain some influence at the court, Artus Désiré addressed his little "libelle" to Charles IX in 1568. Its direct influence is unknown, as there is no proof that it was ever read by the monarch. Four years later, however, at a moment when Protestant leaders were again circulating freely in Paris and throughout much of the nation, Désiré's principal recommendation to the king was carried out in the massacre of Saint-Barthélemy. In 1571 Désiré began publishing again in Paris, and there were no further signs of royal displeasure.

III

Born early in the century, deceased about 1580 if not later; possibly from Normandy and certainly a priest; a literary career lasting from 1545 to 1586; involved in a plot against the government of Charles IX, and sentenced to a prison term which he did not serve; these are among the few certain facts of his biography. But a scrutiny of his works makes possible a few other conjectures regarding his activities, and some conclusions about his way of life.

"Il paraît," observed Niceron, ".... que la nécessité lui mettoit souvent la plume à la main, et qu'il y cherchoit une ressource pour les besoins de la vie." [34] He was certainly poor. In the *Grans abus et barbouilleries* he displayed an intimate acquaintance with low-class tavern life; and from certain lines it would seem that he may have depended for his sustenance on the free food and wine he felt were due his ecclesiastical status, in exchange for a "patenostre." [35] And no doubt he hoped for some reward from his writings, some of which, peripheral to his main purpose, may have been pot-boilers.[36] "Il est clair," added Goujet, "... qu'il ne

---

[34] Niceron, loc. cit.
[35] See the analysis of that pamphlet in chap. III of this work.
[36] For example, the *Grans abus et barbouilleries* just mentioned.

possédoit aucun bénéfice, mais qu'il n'eût pas été fâché d'en avoir." [37] His often expressed hatred of plurality of benefices in unworthy hands, coupled with his dismay that deserving clerics were often left destitute of any charge, supports this conjecture. [38] However, it must be admitted that economic necessity never led him to compromise his principles in his published works; on the contrary, few writers, even in his impassioned age, equaled the single-minded fanaticism with which he pursued his life-long goal: total extirpation of the protestant heresy from France. The risking of his life for his cause places his sincerity, if not his good sense, beyond question. In the *Comédie du pape malade*, Artus Désiré is portrayed as a venal hack, serving "mère Eglise" primarily for the financial reward; [39] but such a partisan source is subject to caution, and the implication may be unjust.

In the same work, he is depicted as being of an irascible and violent disposition. [40] This trait conforms not only to the picture that stands out from his writings, almost all showing a violent temperament, but also to what we know of one of his favorite associates, Maître François Picard. [41] Varillas described him as an "homme extraordinairement licentieux," but this trait is unconfirmed by other sources. [42] Finally Brunet voiced the theory that his mind was deranged; [43] but again, there is no evidence,

---

[37] Goujet, op. cit., p. 130.

[38] See the analysis of his works, chap. III of this work, for confirmation.

[39] Badius, *La Comédie du pape malade*, lines 1277-8, 1345-8, in which *L'Affamé* declares:

> Quoy? me voyla en ma chemise
> Pour avoir servi mere Eglise....
> J'aimerois mieux un Tien contant
> Qu'un Tu l'auras valant autant
> Ou dix fois plus à advenir.
> Il n'est rien tel que de tenir....

[40] Ibid., lines 1273-76:

> Et *dea, magister* Desiré,
> *Vos estis bene* choleré.
> Je disois que deviendrois sage
> Apres avoir esté en cage....

[41] See below, this chap., for remarks about Fr. Picard.

[42] Varillas, loc. cit. See below, Chap. II, under *Passevent parisien* (X) for possible explanation of the comment by Varillas.

[43] Brunet, loc. cit.

beyond his fanaticism and lack of organization, to support this conjecture.

How much did he travel? Twice he announced that Henri II had sent him on pilgrimage to Notre Dame de Lorette.[44] In addition, it is possible that during his period of silence between 1553 and 1558, he traveled to Geneva: after the latter date the life of the Genevans occupied an important place in his works which it had not had before. He implied at that time that his reports were based on his own observation; and he claimed to be the author of the *Passevent parisien*, a pamphlet in prose purporting to describe at first hand the profligate conduct of the leaders of the Genevan Church.[45] Perhaps his interest in Geneva stemmed from his own travels; but it may be that by the end of the reign of Henri II Geneva had become, much more than before, the focus of clerical attacks from France, and that Désiré was merely following the new fashion.[46] This matter is hardly clarified by a 1550 preface in which he claimed to have visited Geneva, and by a 1561 preface in which he said that he hadn't.[47]

IV

Some additional light is shed on his character and temperament by the company he kept. His clerical ideal seems to have been embodied in a certain François Picard, docteur de Sorbonne, for the first anniversary of whose death he composed a eulogy, published in 1557. François Picard is first mentioned by the

---

[44] Once in the *Contrepoison* (see my bibliography of his works, Chap. II of this work) in several editions of which he included a prayer "Oraison que l'autheur a fait a Nostre Dame de L'aurette," etc.; again in his *requeste à la Royne mere*, quoted above.

[45] See my discussion of the authorship of *Passevent parisien*, chap. III below.

[46] Du Bellay's sonnets on the subject, and the ensuing exchange, are only one indication of such a trend during the last years of the reign of Henri II.

[47] All editions of the *Combatz du fidele papiste*, from 1550 onward carry an "An lecteur" in which he describes in great detail the dilapidated condition of the church of St. Pierre in Geneva. On the other hand, in the preface to the *Hymnes en françois* of 1561, he defers for firsthand information to those who have been there.

Histoire ecclésiastique in 1553 in a reference to "ceux de Sorbone, et notamment le Docteur Béda, et un autre nommé Picard, Parisien, jeune pour lors, mais d'un esprit tempestif, s'il y en eut jamais, et qui depuis a esté tenu pour un des principaux pilliers de l'Eglise Romaine." [48] He makes several other appearances in the *Histoire ecclésiastique*, usually in the role of a vindictive hounder of heretics. Following the execution of fourteen Huguenots at Meaux, "... le lendemain, Picard, pour achever son triomphe, venu avec une magnifique procession en la place où le feu ardoit encores ... dit entre autres choses, après s'estre bien tempesté, qu'il estoit necessaire à salut de croire que ces quatorze executés estoient damnés au fond des enfers, et que si un ange du ciel venoit dire du contraire il le faudroit rejetter, pource que Dieu ne seroit point Dieu, s'il ne les damnoit eternellement...." [49]

On another occasion, "un nommé Seraphin.... fut surpris, et avec quatre autres bruslé à Paris avec une admirable constance, en laquelle advint cela de notable, que Picard estant tout esperdu, au lieu de despiter et tempester comme il avoit accoustumé de faire en tels cas, se meist à exhorter à patience l'un des cinq, lequel d'un visage riant luy dit ces mots, si haut qu'ils furent entendus aisement, Monsieur nostre maistre, loué soit Dieu, que vous changés de langage, mais si vous estiés à ma place oseriez-vous vous vanter d'avoir si bonne patience que celle que Dieu me donne? Et ainsi moururent ces cinq martyrs." [50] It is not without significance that Désiré in his memorial volume, praised Picard for the very qualities noted by the author of the *Histoire ecclésiastique*.

Another colleague with whom Artus Désiré seems to have been on good terms, was Jacques Guéset, "Curé de Sainct Paterne homme de mesme humeur que luy....," [51] with whom he stayed in Orléans before leaving on his mission to Spain. This priest came to a violent end, for on July 31, 1562, when the city of Orléans was occupied by Condé's troops, "le Curé de Sainct Paterne d'Orléans (qui s'estoit tenu caché en un grenier depuis le com-

---

[48] *Hist. ecclés.*, I, 26-27.
[49] Ibid., 69-70.
[50] Ibid., 72-73.
[51] Ibid., 813.

mencement de ceste guerre, homme tres meschant et complice de la conjuration contre le Roy et le Royaume de laquelle Artus Désiré avoit esté trouvé saisi....) fut pendu et estranglé en la place nommée le Martroy, mourant comme une vraye beste qu'il estait." [52] Another detail about this priest is furnished by N. Weiss, who reports that "ce n'est pas comme curé, ni comme espion ou fabricant de fausse monnaie qu'il fut executé, mais comme complice d'Artus Désiré qui avait été surpris allant de la part des Parisiens, supplier Philippe II de rétablir l'ordre en France." [53]

* * *

Despite this meager information on the life of Artus Désiré, the essential character and personality of the man stand out clearly. Of humble origin and limited intelligence, he devoted his life to defending the faith in which he had been raised. He distinguished himself less for his intellectual qualities than for the violence and intransigeance of his attitude. He does not appear to have prospered during his lifetime; and since his own period there has been no one, even among his co-religionists to defend his case with any warmth.

Beyond the few facts and conjectures offered here, his career can be traced by his published works. These will be listed, as completely as possible, in the next chapter.

---

[52] Ibid., 147-8.
[53] Weiss, N., Review in *BSHPF*, Vol. 49 (1900), p. 652 of Lacombe, Bernard de, *Les débuts des guerres de religion, Orléans, 1559-1564*.

Chapter II

BIBLIOGRAPHY OF EDITIONS OF THE WORKS OF ARTUS DÉSIRÉ

The accompanying list of works and editions of Artus Désiré is the result of a search, in person and by mail, of the principal libraries of Paris, of a number of other libraries in France and elsewhere, and of other bibliographical sources both usual and less known. The most complete listing of Désiré's editions is to be found in J. C. Brunet, *Manuel du libraire et de l'amateur de livres*, edition of 1861, and the *Supplement* to it, by G. Brunet and Deschamps. These two works between them cite over sixty editions of his various pamphlets, but omit any mention of several of them. On the other hand, A. Cioranesco in his *Bibliographie de la littérature francaise du XVIe siècle*, while giving a more complete list of his various works, includes reference to only about forty different editions.

The present list runs to over 100 editions of his works, and is still probably not complete. Investigation of the resources of additional libraries would surely demonstrate the existence of several others. I do not know the source of the remark in the *Dictionnaire de biographie française* that those of his works held by the Bibliotheque Nationale "ne représenteraient qu'une infime partie de la production de Désiré, s'il est vrai que celui-ci a publié plus de 200 pièces."

Inevitably in a listing of 16th century material, the quality of the references is unequal. Ideally the bibliographer would like to examine each edition cited. Practically, of course, this is impossible. In the present instance, many of the editions have been examined. But even more have not. In most cases the references to those not examined personally are so clear and exact as to be considered absolutely trustworthy. Unfortunately, from a rating of excellent, they run the whole range down to a few which must be admitted unsure, and to one or two which are highly suspect. But because of the astonishing number and diversity of good references, I have hesitated to dismiss any outright.

In listing my sources, I have used the entries in Brunet as a base, and have supplied other information either when I have found a copy of the edition, or when the edition does not appear in Brunet's listing.

I have tried to keep this bibliography as simple and uncomplicated as possible. The following observations may help to clarify the method used.

1. The separate works are listed, under roman numerals, in chronological order of their first publication, with subsequent editions of the same work listed chronologically after the first edition.
2. This classification has then been retained in chapter III, where contents of the various works are analyzed separately.
3. The arabic numerals to the left of each entry run consecutively through all editions, and serve as overall reference numbers.
4. A few editions were published between January 1 and March 25, and show the date of the preceding year, sometimes stating "avant Pâques", for example, no. 2 in my listing. In such cases I have retained the date of the title page and placed the words "old style" in parentheses directly beneath.

I.

1. 1545 *Lamentation de nostre mere saincte Eglise, sur les contradictions des Heretiques, suivant l'erreur des faulx defectueux.*

Paris   Veuve de Pierre   Brunet
Vidoue

In verse. No other information on this little work, whose existence is clearly attested by Brunet and others. It is not difficult to guess at its contents, since several of his other early works contain sections on the same subject:

1) 1550 *Deffensoire* opens with a lament by the church;
2) 1550 *Combats* contains in all editions a final section entitled *Complaincte de la susdite eglise contre lesdictz Heretiques ennemys de la foy.*
3) 1553 *Desespoir testamentaire* likewise contains a passage in which the church airs her grievances against the heretics.

II.

2. 1546 *Le Miroer des francs Taulpins, autrement dictz Antechristz, et de la nouvelle alliance du tresmiserable et reprouvé Luther.*
   (old style)

   Paris   Jehan André   Brunet

   48 ff. not numbered, round type; "fait et composé." Dated 1546, but the privilege is as of "le vingt deuxiesme jour de Mars, l'an mil cinq cens quarante six avant Paques," therefore 1547 (new style). This work consists of 10-syllable lines in rhymed couplets, covering a number of the points at issue between the protestants and catholics, from the most orthodox catholic viewpoint.

3. 1546 *Le Miroer des Francs Taulpins,* etc.
   (old style)

Paris　　　Jehan André　　　Brunet
　　　　　　　　　　　　　　Ste. Geneviève:
　　　　　　　　　　　　　　D8°4285 (pièce 1)
　　　　　　　　　　　　　　Rés.

Same as preceding edition, except for words "nouvellement reveu et corrigé." Same date. Dedicated to "tresreverend pere en Dieu, monseigneur d'Augiers." This and the following edition contain a final ballad, beginning

> Si vous voulez parfaittement
> Cognoistre à l'œil un Heretique ....

whose refrain is "Comme deux chiens après un os." This ballad figures in the Rasse des Nœux manuscripts as an independent composition under the title "La Touche d'Artus Désiré."

4. 1547 *Le Miroir des francz Taulpins,* etc.

　　Paris　　　Jehan André　　　Goujet Versailles:
　　　　　　　　　　　　　　　　　8°92

Same as preceding edition, except for "1547" on title page.

5. 1547 *Deffensoire de la foy chrestienne.*

　　Paris　　　Jehan André　　　Brunet

Brunet does not give full information on this edition or on No. 7 below. See No. 9 for full title. The entire text of the *Miroer* is incorporated into the *Deffensoire*, which is expanded to about twice the length of the other, probably earlier, work. The *Deffensoire* is likewise better organized: it treats all the same questions, plus a number of others, but is clearly divided into chapters by subject.

6. 1548 *Deffensoire*, etc.

   Paris   Jehan André   Nantes: Musée Dobrée.

   Same, except for date.

7. 1549 *Deffensoire*, etc., *avec le Miroer des Francs Taulpins*.

   Rouen   Du Gort frères   Brunet

   No other information.

8. no date *Le Miroir des francs taupins, autrement dictz Antechristz, Auquel est contenu le deffensoire de la foy chrestienne. Avec plusieurs figures nouvellement augmentées.*

   Rouen   Du Gort frères   B. Nationale: Rés. p. Ye 387

   40 ff. not numbered; small type. Despite the title, this is the original text of the *Miroer*, without the *Deffensoire*. It is possibly the earliest Rouen edition, and contains a fine set of woodcut illustrations, which had not appeared in the earlier Paris editions.

9. 1550 *Le Deffensoire de la Foy Chrestienne, contenant en soy le Miroer des Francs Taupins, autrement nommez Lutheriens, nouvellement augmenté et corrigé, oultre les precedentes impressions.*

   Rouen   Du Gort frères   Arsenal: 8°BL 10.837 (Rés.)

   80 ff. not numbered. Same woodcuts as No. 8. Dedicated to "Monseigneur Durant à Serta, second president en la court de parlement de Tholosa."

10. 1552 *Le Deffensoire de la foy chrestienne, contenant en soy le Miroer des errantz autrement dit Lutheriens*, etc.

Lyon   Jean Pullon,   Brunet
        dit de Trin

84 ff. including 5 preliminary.

11. 1554 *Miroir des francs taupins.... Nouvellement composé par A. D. P.*

    Paris   Jean Ruelle   Brunet
                            Goujet

    According to Goujet, there are 27 chapters, each preceded by a woodcut. This would make of it a different work, distinct both from earlier editions of the *Miroer*, which had no chapter divisions, and from the *Deffensoire*, which had 18 distinct chapters.

12. 1564 *Deffensoire de la foy chrestienne avec le Miroir*, etc.

    Paris   Jean Ruelle   Brunet

13. 1567 *Deffensoire*, etc. with *Miroer*.

    Paris   Jean Ruelle   B. Nationale:
                            Rés. Ye. 1864

    80 ff. not numbered; "nouvellement composé" on the title page, but actually the same work.

14. no date *Miroir des francs Taupins.*

    Angers   (no publisher given) Goujet

    No other information.

III.

15. 1550 *Les Combatz du fidelle papiste pelerin romain, contre l'apostat priapiste, tirant à la synagogue de Geneve, maison babilonique des Lutheriens. Ensemble*

la Description de la cité de Dieu, assiégée des Heretiques. Le tout composé par Artus Desiré. Avec privilege.

Rouen   Du Gort frères   B. Nationale:
Rés. p. Ye 228 (1)

141 ff. not numbered. Despite the title, the *Description* is missing from this volume. See No. 16 below. Dedicated "Au trespuissant et treschrestien Roy Henry deuxiesme de ce nom..." with a poem of eleven lines beginning "Prince sacré de tous Roys le plus digne..."

16. 1550   *La Description de la cité de Dieu. Figurée à nostre mere Saincte Eglise, assiegée des malheureux hereticques qui se sont levez contre elle devers Midi, Orient, Occident et Septentrion, Avec l'assault des fidelles Chrestiens appellez pour deffendre la dite cité. Ensemble aussi la complaincte de la susdite eglise contre lecdictz Heretiques ennemys de la foy.*

Rouen   Du Gort frères   B. Nationale:
Rés. p. Ye 228 (2)

34 ff. not numbered; signatures scratched out, but probably continued those of *Combatz* (No. 15) above, indicating a single edition of 175 ff. Both volumes are richly illustrated with woodcuts, including some from the *Deffensoire*.

17. 1550   *Les Combatz du fidelle Papiste pelerin Romain, Contre l'apostat Antipapiste tirant à la Synagogue de Geneve, maison babilonicque des Lutheriens. Reveu et corrigé par l'auteur. Ensemble la Description de la cité.... etc. Le tout composé par Artus Désiré.*

Rouen   Du Gort frères   Arsenal:
8°BL 10.838

141 ff. Title and two pages of prefatory material are unnumbered; following ff. are numbered 3-140. Despite the title, the *Description* is again missing.

18. 1551 *Les Combatz du Fidelle Chrestien, dit Papiste, contre l'Infidelle apostat anti Papiste Reveu et corrigé par l'autheur. Ensemble la description de la Cité de Dieu assiegée des heretiques. Le tout composé par Artus Désiré. Au treschrestien Roy Henry II.*

| Lyon | Jean Pullon, dit de Trin | Brunet Br. Museum: C.70.a. 10 |

165 ff. with woodcuts. This is the earliest edition listed by Brunet.

19. 1552 *Les Combatz,* etc. *Ensemble la Description,* etc.

| Rouen | Du Gort frères | B. Nationale: 8°Z. Don. 594. (5) |

175 ff. numbed recto only to 141, that is, to the end of the *Combatz*. The *Description*, which this time is bound in the same volume, is here listed separately as No. 20, since it appears to have been part of a different édition.

20. 1550 *La Description de la cité de Dieu,* etc. *Ensemble aussi la Complaincte,* etc.

| Rouen | Du Gort frères | B. Nationale: 8°A. Don. 594 (5) |

34 ff. not numbered. Although bound with *Combatz* of 1552, and continuing the signatures of that edition, these ff. appear to have been part of a different edition. There is a new title page at the head of this section, dated 1550; and the folio numbers are missing. Nor is this the same edition of the *Description* as

No. 16 above, also dated 1550, since there are slight differences of alignment on the title page:

No. 16 "Ensemble aussi la complaincte de la susdite egli-/se contre lesdictz Heretiques ennemys de la foy.

No. 20 "Ensemble aussi la complaincte de la susdi-/te Eglise, contre lesdictz Heretiques enne-/mys de la Foy.

The fact that a *Description* of 1550 is bound with a *Combatz* of 1552, and that this *Description* has its own complete title page, is evidence that from the beginning the *Description* had some degree of independence of the *Combatz*. But the words "Ensemble aussi" instead of merely "Ensemble" in the title of the *Description*, together with its signatures, indicate its basic role as a part of the Combatz.

21. 1553 *Les Batailles et Victoires du Chevalier Celeste, contre le Chevalier Terrestre.*

    Paris   Magdeleine Boursette   Brunet
Br. Museum: C.39.a.65

175 ff. 29 vignettes sur bois. See No. 23 below for discussion of this title.

22. 1554 *Batailles et victoires*, etc.

    Paris   Jehan Ruelle   Viollet-le-Duc, *Catalogue*

No other information on this edition.

23. 1554 *Les Combatz du Celeste Chrestien dit Papiste pelerin Romain, contre l'Apostat terrestre Antipapiste tirant à*

la sinagogue de Geneve, maison babilonique des Lutheriens. Ensemble la Description de la cité de Dieu, etc.

Paris	Magdeleine Boursette	Brunet
		Arsenal: 8°BL 10.840

175 ff. numbered recto only; woodcuts. In all probability a reissue of No. 21 above, this edition shows an inconsistency in title. As indicated above, the title page gives a variation of the usual title of *Combatz*. But the text is headed by a new title: *Les Batailles et victoires du chevalier Celeste, contre le chevalier Terrestre,* which was the title-page title of the 1553 edition from the same press. In like manner, the title page gives the usual title of *Description*, but this text, starting on folio 144R, is entitled: *Les terribles et merveilleux assaulx, donnez contre la saincte cité de Hierusalem, figurée a nostre mere saincte Eglise, environnée des ennemys de la foy.* The text of both sections is identical with earlier editions. All subsequent Paris editions will consist of 175 ff. with the new title. But at least two more editions appeared outside of Paris under the old title.

24. 1555 *Combats du fidele papiste.*

Lyon   Jean Temporel   Brunet
       (on title page)
       Jacques Faure
       (on last page)

165 ff. woodcuts.

25. 1556. *Combats du fidele papiste.*

Rouen   (publisher not given) Goujet

26. 1557 *Les Batailles et victoires.*

      Paris   Jehan Ruelle   Brunet
      Br. Museum: C.39.a.64

      175 ff. "nouvellement reveu."

27. 1559 *Les Terribles et merveilleux assauts,* etc.

      Paris   Pierre Gaultier   Mazarine: 25.221 (pièce)

      32 ff. Complete text of the second part of this work, previously listed as No. 16 and No. 20 under title *Description de la cité de Dieu.* In this edition the signatures start with A.

28. 1560 *Batailles et victoires,* etc.

      Paris   Jehan Ruelle   Brunet
      B. Nationale: Rés. Ye 326
      B. Protestantisme R4214

      175 ff. Italic type. Same woodcuts.

29. 1561 *Batailles et victoires,* etc.

      Paris   Jehan Ruelle   Genève: Bibliothèque publique et universitaire

30. 1562 *Batailles et victoires,* etc.

      Paris   Jehan Ruelle   Genève: E. Droz

31. 1562 *Batailles et victoires,* etc.

      Paris   Estienne Grouleau   Brunet

32. 1562 *Terribles et merveilleux assauts.*

    Paris   Pierre Gaultier   Brunet

    31 ff.

33. 1570 *Batailles et victoires*, etc.

    Paris   Jehan Ruelle   Brunet
                                                        B. Nationale: Rés.
                                                        Ye. 1866

    175 ff. Roman type. Same woodcuts.

34. 1570 *Batailles et victoires*, etc.

    Paris   Jehan Ruelle   Br. Museum: 11474.
                      le jeune   a.17

    175 ff. Roman type. No apparent difference from the preceding entry except name of publisher.

35. 1585 *Batailles et victoires*, etc.

    Paris   Veuve Jehan   Arsenal:
                      Ruelle   8°BL 10.843

    175 ff. Same woodcuts.

36. 1586 *Batailles et victoires*, etc.

    Paris   Veuve Jehan   Brunet
                      Ruelle   Rouen: 6296 (2g)
                                                        B. Protestantisme:
                                                        13911

    175 ff. The copy in the Bibliothèque du Protestantisme lacks title page, but the catalogue lists it as of 1586.

37. no date   *Batailles et victoires,* etc.

      Paris   Louys de Mesnil   Brunet
                                                    B. Protestantisme:
                                                      (André) 324
                                                     Ste Geneviève:
                                                     Y.8°1134 Inv.2564
                                                            Rés.

      276 pp.; probably relatively late.

IV.

38. 1550   *Loyauté conscientieuse des taverniers.*

      Paris   Nicolas Buffet   La Croix du Maine

      Neither the date 1550 nor the masculine form "taverniers" appears in any other references. According to Goujet (III, 134-5), this work, "qui est de 1550, est en dizains, et chaque dizain y est suivi d'un quatrain en vers de cinq syllabes. L'exemplaire in-16 n'a que 37 ff.: il est en lettres italiques, sans nom d'auteur, et sans marque de lieu ni d'année."

39. no date   *Loyanté conscientieuse des tavernieres.*

      no place   no publisher   Goujet
                                                                     Brunet

40. 1578   *Les grans abus et barbouilleries des taverniers et tavernieres, qui meslent et brouillent le vin. Avec la feinte reception et ruse des Hostesses et chambrieres envers leurs Hostes. Plus une reformation des Taverniers et gourmandise.*

      Rouen   Nicolas Lescuyer   Brunet
                                                                     B. Nationale: Rés.
                                                                     Ye. 1933

93 pp. alternating 10-line stanzas of 10 syllable-lines, with 4-line stanzas of 5 syllable lines. Although clearly a reedition of the *Loyauté conscientieuse,* this volume would seem to contain additional material.

V.

41. 1551 *Les grands jours du Parlement de Dieu, Publiez par monsieur sainct Mathieu, ou tous Chrestiens sont adjournez à comparoistre en personne pour respondre sur les grans blasphemes, tromperies, et deceptions du regne qui court, qui sont les terribles et merveilleux sigens de l'Antechrist, Par Artus Desiré.*

Rouen	Du Gort frères	Brunet
		Arsenal: 8°BL 10.839
		(Rés.)

40 ff. not numbered. Dedicated "A tous vrays Chrestiens et fidelles." Composed exclusively in 10-line stanzas, ABABBCCDCD, of 10-syllable lines.

42. 1564 *Grands jours du Parlement de Dieu.*

Paris (publisher not given) Cioranesco

43. 1574 *Grands jours du Parlement de Dieu.*

Paris   Anthoine Hoüic   Brunet

44. 1615 *Grands jours du Parlement de Dieu.*

Paris   Belley   Brunet

VI.

45. 1553 *Hymnes ecclesiastiques, traduits en ryme françoyse sur les memes chants.*

| | | Rouen | Du Gort frères | Du Verdier |
| | | | | Brunet |

46. 1561 *Hymnes en françois sur le chant de ceux de l'Eglise, à l'honneur de Dieu et de tous les Sainctz et Sainctes de Paradis.*

    Paris   Jehan Ruelle   Brunet
                                             Arsenal: 8°BL 10.463
                                             (Rés.)

120 ff. not numbered. A woodcut precedes each hymn as far as folio 60. Dedicated to "Monseigneur Monseigneur l'evesque d'Aucerre" in a 10-line poem. According to Brunet, these hymns are the same as the *Hymnes ecclesiastiques* above. In addition to the hymns of the title, which go only to folio 81, the volume contains a "Prologue exhortatif au fidele Chrestien," a diatribe against "plusieurs gens mal sentant de la foy", some "Chansons spirituelles" on popular songs of the day, a long prose sermon, and a "Table des hymnes."

47. no date *Les Himnes en françoys sur le chant de ceux de l'Eglise.*

    Troyes   Nicolas Oudot   Brunet
                                               Arsenal: 8°BL 10.465

120 ff. numbered recto only to 76, thereafter not numbered. The contents of this volume are almost the same as for preceding edition, but two short pieces are added before the *Table*, "De la necessité d'obeyr à Dieu" and "Comment rendra au dernier jour à chacun selon ses oeuvres."

48. 1561 *Plaisans et armonieux cantiques de devotion, composez sur le chant des Hymnes de nostre Mere saincte Eglise, à la louange de Dieu et de ses Sainctz,*

qui est un second Contrepoison aux cinquante deux Chansons de Clement Marot, Par Artus Desiré.

Paris   Pierre Gaultier   Brunet
B. Nationale: 8°Ye. 6115

63 ff. numbered recto only. Dedicated to "Messieurs les Venerables Vicaires et Chantres de nostre Dame de Paris." Probably because of the words "second Contrepoison" this work has been associated with the work entitled "Contrepoison" by Désiré. In actual fact, the *cantiques* here published are identical with the *hymnes*, except that seven of the latter are not included in this collection. The "Prologue exhortatif" is largely the same as the various editions of the *hymnes:* but the other supplementary pieces to the *hymnes* are missing from this edition.

49. 1576 *Hymnes chrestiens en françois en ryme.*

Rouen   Th. Reinsart   Brunet

Woodcuts.

50. 1580 *Hymnes en françois sur le chant de ceux de l'Eglise.*

Paris   Nicolas Bonfons   Brunet
Arsenal: 8°BL 10.464 (Rés.)

120 ff. not numbered. Contents the same as 1561 edition of *hymnes*, including dedication to the "evesque d'Aucerre."

VII.

51. 1553 *Instruction crestienne contre les execrables blasphemes et Blasphemateurs du nom de Dieu, et autres*

pechez qui regnent à present, Composé par Artus Desiré.

| Paris | Veuve François Regnault | Brunet Arsenal: 8°BL 10.841 |

72 pp. Dedicated to "Tresvenerable et tresreverend pere en Dieu, Monseigneur, monsieur l'archevesque de Bourges." The work consists of 8-line stanzas, 8-syllable lines; ABABBCBC. Included with the title work are "De l'ingratitude des mauvais riches et de la charité que devons avoir aux pauvres," and "De mauvais exemple que les peres et meres donnent à leurs enfans de perdition."

52. 1558 *Instruction chrestienne contre les execrables blasphemes et blasphemateurs du nom de Dieu et autres pechez qui regnent à present. Plus les merveilleuses et admirables revelations que saint Jean eut en l'isle de Pathmos, selon le texte de l'Apocalypse.*
Le tout composé par Artus Desiré.

| Lyon | Benoist Rigaud et Jan Saugrain | Cioranesco Toulouse: Rés. D. XVI 157 |

VIII.

53. 1553 *Le Desespoir testamentaire de l'enfant de perdition, chef de l'Eglise maligne. Avec ses lamentations et complainctes. Imprimé à Rouen pour Artus Desiré Auteur de ce present livre.*

| Rouen | no publisher | Mazarine: 20.857 |

16 ff. numbered by hand recto only, 153-168. Dedicated to "tresvenerable et Religieuse personne frere Pierre Sardé prieur des Chartreux de Cahors en

quercy." Rhymed couplets of 8-syllable lines. The child in question is Martin Luther. Cioranesco lists an edition of 1553 without city of publication. However his reference is probably to this same volume in the Bibliothèque Mazarine: the files of Emile Picot list the Mazarine copy, including its *cote de magasin,* but not the city of publication.

IX.

54. 1554 *Premier (et second) livre de la description philosophale de la nature et condition des animaux.*

Paris   Magdeleine Boursette   Brunet

Brunet adds: "Les moralités sont de Artus Désiré." An earlier work called *Decades de la description, forme et vertu naturelle des animaux, tant raisonnables que brutes,* containing no moralities, and written by Barthélemy Aneau, was published anonymously in 1549 by B. Arnoullet, Lyon, and itself underwent several editions under the title *Decades de la description,* etc., and also as *La description, forme et nature des bestes tant privées que sauvaiges, avec le pourtret et figure, au plus pres du naturel.* (Rouen, Robert et Jehan du Gort,1554.) The present volume is apparently the earliest to carry the little poems added by Désiré to Aneau's work. The "second livre" does for the birds what the first book does for the animals.

55. 1561 *La description philosophale, etc., des bestes, avec sens moral.*

no place   no publisher   Br. Museum: 976.c.4 (1)

56. 1568 *Description philosophale*, etc.

        Paris   Jehan Ruel   Brunet
                  (Ruelle)

        Woodcuts. Brunet does not give the whole title, but lists this edition under *Description philosophale*, which implies the inclusion of Désiré's moralities.

57. 1568 *Le premier livre de la description philosophique de la nature et condition des animaux, tant raisonnables que brutz, avec le sens moral comprins sur la nature et condition d'iceux: augmenté de divers et estranges bestes.*

        Lyon   Jean d'Ogerolles   Brunet

        Woodcuts.

58. 1571 *Description philosophale forme et nature des bestes, tant privées que sauvages avec le sens moral compris sur la natuer et condition d'iceux.*

        Paris   Jehan Ruelle   Brunet
                                                 Br. Museum: 727.b. 23(1) &(2)

        48 ff. with woodcuts. The volume also contains *Description Philosophale des oyseaux, et de l'inclination et proprieté d'iceux*. (Paris, Jehan Ruelle, 1571.)

59. 1581 *Description philosophale*, 1) *des bestes*, and 2) *des oyseaux*, etc.

        Paris   Nicolas Bonfons   Brunet

        22 ff. Same text as 1571 edition, but joined to the *Blason des fleurs*. (Brunet).

60. 1605 *Le premier livre de la description,* etc.

Paris   (no publisher given) Brunet

48 ff. with woodcuts.

61. 1641 *La description philosophale forme, et manière des Bestes, et des Oyseaux, tant privez que sauvages. Avec le sens moral comprins sur le naturel et condition d'iceux.*

Rouen   David Ferrand   Arsenal: 8°S.8432

96 pp. plus 96 pp. This is the only edition I have seen. The first half of the volume deals with animals, the second with birds. There is a wood cut illustration for each creature described. The original work apparently consisted, for each animal, of an 8-line stanza, 8-syllables per line, of description, plus a more elaborate prose analysis of the character and appearance of the animal. Désiré's contribution was to insert another 8-line stanza explaining the symbolic meaning of each animal and bird.

X.

62. 1556 *Passevent parisien respondant a Pasquin Romain, de la vie de ceux qui sont allez demourer, et se disent vivre selon la reformation de l'Evangile, au pais jadis de Savoye: et maintenant soubz les Princes de Berne, et Seigneurs de Geneve: faict en forme de Dialogue.*

no place   no publisher   B. Nationale: Rés.Z. 4010

48 ff. numbered recto only. A note in brown ink on the title page of this copy offers the following comment: "A Lyon, par Artus Desiré, touchant lequel voyez M. de Thou... et Varillas... histoire de Charles IX page 129, qui a pourtant tres mal entendu

M. de Thou quand il a traduit profligans pudoris homo, homme d'une vie extraordinairement licentieuse, au lieu de traduire homme resolu jusqu'a l'imprudence. Du Verdier... (dans) sa Bibliotheque attribue ce dialogue à Antoine Cathalan contre lequel Calvin a ecrit." For a discussion of this disputed authorship, see Chapter III below, where it is concluded that Cathalan and not Désiré is the author. This is one of at least seven editions of this little dialogue in prose, all published in 1556. It is impossible to establish their chronological order. The work contains a preface, entitled "Passevent faisant son Proeme." The text is a slanderous recital of the alleged lubricity of the Huguenot leaders of Geneva. As the title suggests, it is an attempt to answer the *Epistola Magistri Benedicti Passavanti* of Théodore de Bèze.

63. 1556 *Passevent parisien respondant à Pasquin romain*, etc.

   Lyon   no publisher   Mazarine: 23.120 (pièce)

   45 ff. numbered recto only. This copy is bound after the *Passavanti* of de Bèze, to which it was clearly intended as a reply.

64. 1556 *Passevent parisien respondant à Pasquin romain*, etc.

   Lyon   no publisher   Brunet

   According to Brunet, "L'édition de Lyon, 1556 in 16 porte le nom de maistre Antoine Cathalan." It must be distinct from the preceding Lyon edition, No. 63 above, which gives no name of the author.

65. 1556 *Passevent parisien respondant à Pasquin romain*, etc.

   Paris   Veuve Nicolas Buffet   B. Nationale: D. 21973

This volume begins with an "Epistre au Lecteur Chrestien. Selon le dire du sage Salomon, etc." which is not included in the other editions I have seen.

66. 1556 *Passevent parisien respondant à Pasquin romain,* etc.
     Paris   G. Guillard   Barbier

67. 1556 *Passevent parisien respondant à Pasquin romain,* etc.
     Paris   no publisher   Geneva, Bibliothèque publique & universitaire

Instead of the name of the publisher, this volume gives the words "à l'enseigne de la vigne." This was a formula generally used by Pierre Gaultier.

68. 1556 *Passevent parisien respondant à Pasquin romain,* etc.
     Toulouse   Henry Marèchal   Barbier

69. 1875 *Passevent parisien respondant à Pasquin romain,* etc.
     Paris   I. Liseux

Liseux published this volume as a companion to his edition of the *Passavanti* of de Bèze of the same year. He included the *Epistre* which had appeared earlier in the Paris, Buffet edition.

*

The year 1556 also saw publication of a little work entitled *Le Double des lettres envoyées à Passevent parisien, par le noble et excellent Pasquin Romain, contenant en vérité la vie de Jehan Calvin,* Paris, Pierre Gaultier. Although it purports to be a continuation of the *Passevent parisien,* this little book resembles in style neither the *Passevent* nor Désiré's usual verse. It probably represents an attempt by a like-minded author, to capitalize on the success of the original work. It consists of 12 ff. of 10-syllable couplets.

XI.

70. 1556 *Exemplaire et probation de jeûne et abstinence de la chair. Avec la mort et passion des saints Machabées.*

    Paris   Magdeleine Boursette   Goujet

"Cet ouvrage est en prose." (Goujet, XIV, 425.) I have not seen this work, which is not listed by Brunet or Cioranesco among the works of Désiré.

XII

71. 1557 *Les Regretz et complainctes de Passepartout, et Bruitquicourt, sur la memoire renouvellée du trespas et bout de l'an de feu tresnoble et venerable personne Maistre Françoys Picart, docteur en theologie, et grand doyen de Saint Germain de l'Auxerroys. Sutra Erised.*

    Paris   Pierre Gaultier   Brunet
                                           B. Nationale: Rés.p. Ye.151

16 ff not numbered. The signature "Sutra Erised" is a transparent anagram of "Artus Désiré." Dedicated to "Messeigneurs les Prevosts, Echevins et Bourgeoys de la ville de Paris." Composed in rhymed couplets of 8-syllable lines. This little work, in a style unfamiliar to him, was probably inspired by another on the same subject, published anonymously one year earlier, with the title: *Deploration sur le trespas de noble et venerable personne monsieur maistre François Picard, Docteur en Theologie*, etc., *qui mourut à Paris le dixseptiesme jour de Septembre, l'an mil cinq cens cinquante et six.* (Paris, Estienne Denise, 1556.) According to Barbier (I, col. 882): "La Mon-

noye attribue cet ouvrage à Jean d'Aubusson, dont les mots 'dena suasi boni', qui le terminent, forment l'anagramme."

XIII

72. 1558 *Complainte de Paix et de son ami Bontemps.*

| Paris | Hierosme de Gourmont | Brunet B. Nationale: Rés.p. Ye.153 |

7 ff. not numbered. Rhymed couplets, 10-syllable lines, Brunet attributes this opuscule to Désiré on the grounds that the copy he saw is bound with two works which Désire is known to have written: *Regretz et Complainctes de Passepartout* (No. 71 above) and *Regretz, Complainctes,* etc... *d'une demoiselle* (No. 74 below). The verse is poorly enough constructed to be of Désiré's composition, but there are several elements in the poem which seem to preclude him as author. For example, the lines:

> Ariadne fut de Thesee laissée,
> Et mesmement fut translaté es cieux
> Un astre illec par le vouloir des Dieux.
> Iphygenie n'a fait la main prophane
> De son parent pour la Dame Diane, etc.
> (f. 5 verso)

bespeak a familiarity with Greek literature, and a penchant for classical references wholly foreign to Désiré. And whereas *Paix* and *Bontemps* are distressed with the warfare devastating all Europe, Désiré was customarily concerned with trouble within France caused by the religious dissension. The final appeal for "virtue" does not even mention the Catholic faith, another reason for rejecting the authorship of Désiré.

XIV

73. 1558 *Les Grandes Chroniques et annales de Passe par tout, Chroniqueur de Geneve, Avec l'origine de Jean Covin, faucement surnommé Calvin, Ensemble la mort et conversion de Mademoiselle la Budée, Par Artus Désiré.*

    Lyon   Benoist Rigaud & Brunet
              Jean Saugrin   B. Protestantisme: R. 7360

128 pp. numbered 3-128. Dedicated "a la tresdevote et fidele Compagnie Lugdunique, qui par la grace de Dieu n'a choppé contre la Chaire de Pestilence, l'ennemy de nos ennemis. Humble Salut." Composed of 8-syllable lines in rhymed couplets. This work is the subject of a critical article by Alfred Cartier. It is a continuation of the tale of the scandalous behavior of the Genevan leaders, begun in the *Passevent parsien*. It was refuted point by point in a little work entitled *Response au livre d'Artus Désiré, intitulé: Les Grandes Chroniques et Annales de Passepartout, fait par Jacques Bienvenu Citoyen de Geneve.* (Geneva, Jacques Berthet, 1558.)

74. 1558 *Les Regretz, Complainctes, et Lamentations d'une Damoiselle, laquelle s'estoit retirée à Genesve pour vivre en liberté. Avec la conversion d'icelle estant à l'article de la mort. Consolation pour les bons Chrestiens, et example pour les mauvais.*

    Paris   Pierre Gaultier   Brunet
    (Apris)   B. Nationale: Rés.p Ye.152

12 ff. not numbered. This is a verbatim extract from the *Grandes Chroniques* above, except that the name Budée has been carefully suppressed, perhaps to render refutation of the case more difficult.

XV

75. 1558 *Les Articles du Traicté de la Paix, entre Dieu et les hommes, Articulez par Artus Désiré.*

Paris   Pierre Gaultier   B. Nationale: Rés. Ye.1867

12 ff. not numbered. Dedicated to "Monsieur Fizes, Conseiller du Roy, et Secretaire de ses finances." A long *Prologue* (ff. 2-7) is followed by 53 quatrains, AABB or ABAB, in 8-syllable lines, devoted to the same theological questions already treated so copiously by Désiré.

76. 1563 *Les Articles du Traicté de la Pais, entre Dieu et les hommes, Articulez par Artus Désiré.*

no place   no publisher   Brunet
B. Nationale: Rés.p. Ye.325

8 ff. not numbered. Title page says "Selon la coppie imprimée à Paris." A different prologue, followed by the same 53 quatrains, in gothic letters.

XVI

77. 1559 *Les Disputes de Guillot le Porcher, et de la Bergere de S. Denis en France, contre Jehan Calvin Predicant de Genesve, sur la verité de nostre saincte Foy Catholicque, et religion chrestienne: Ensemble la*

Genalogie des Hereticques, et fruictz qui proviennent d'iceux. Avec Privilege du Roy.

Paris   Pierre Gaultier   Brunet
B. Nationale: Rés. Ye.3836

80 ff. numbered recto only, starting with Aiv, from 2-77. Dedicated to "Tresnoble et venerable Seigneur, Monseigneur Felix de Varmond, Abbé de Vallette, et Aulmosnier ordinaire de la Royne." Following a dedicatory poem there is a "Table des Matieres contenues en ce present livre." The text consists of 8-line stanzas, ABABBCBC, mostly of 8-syllable lines, but a few stanzas of 10-syllable lines towards the beginning. The work is a three-way conversation between Guillot, the Bergère and Calvin, in which all the controversial questions of dogma are raised, and Calvin refuted point by point.

Cioranesco alone mentions an edition of 1556, indicating the number of folios as iii - 77 - viii ff. Brunet and others give 1559 as the date of the first edition. Several things point to the Gaultier edition of 1559 as being in fact the earliest.

1) The privilege of the 1559 edition is dated January 9, 1558, and is granted for two years; such privileges were seldom renewed. The existence of an edition two years before the privilege was issued would be extraordinary.

2) The arrangement of pages given by Cioranesco suggests strongly the presence of the *débat* in the final folios. In fact this is almost exactly the distribution of pages in the Gaultier edition of 1560. All other signs indicate that the story of the conversion of the demoiselle was first published as an integral part of the *Grandes chroniques,* then republished both separately, as *Les regretz,* etc.... *d'une demoiselle,* and in altered

form as an appendage of the *Disputes*. In any case, the 1559 edition did not contain the *débat*, and it is unlikely that this unit appeared in 1556, then disappeared in 1559, and reappeared in 1560.

3) In *Le retour de Guillot*, Guillot claims to have "presagé un an devant les troubles ce qui est advenu." This is surely a reference to the earlier work in which his name figured. Looking back from the year 1578, it is more likely that he thought of the "troubles" starting in 1559 or 1560, than in 1557.

78. 1560 *Les Disputes de Guillot le Porcher, etc... Plus adjousté de nouveau le debat d'entre ledict Calvin et Theodore de Baise, touchant la conversion d'une Damoiselle, et lesdites disputes.*

    Paris Pierre Gaultier Brunet
                Mazarine: 25.221

    88 ff. numbered recto only, 2-77 (folio 80), plus 8 ff. not numbered. This is essentially the same as the 1559 edition with the addition of the final section on the "conversion."

79. 1560 *Disputes de Guillot le Porger*, etc.

    Lyon Michel Jove Brunet

80. 1561 *Les Disputes de Guillot le Porcher*, etc.

    Paris Pierre Gaultier Geneva, Bibliothèque publique et universitaire

81. 1568 *Disputes de Guillot le Porcher*, etc.

    Paris Jehan Ruelle Brunet

82. 1569 *Les grands débats.... avec les disputes de Guillot le Porcher contre J. Calvin.*

   Paris   (no publisher given)   H. Shaw
                                                   p. 147 (note)

   No other information on this title.

83. 1580 *Disputes de Guillot le Porcher, etc.... plus adjousté de nouveau le debat,* etc.

   Paris   Veuve Jehan Ruelle   Brunet

   88 ff.

84. 1586 *Disputes de Guillot le Porcher, etc.... plus adjousté de nouveau le debat,* etc.

   Paris   Nicolas Bonfons   B. Nationale: Rés. Z. 2529

   80 ff. numbered recto only, 4-80, plus 8 ff. not numbered.

85. 1604 *Les Disputes,* etc.

   Rouen   Abraham le Cousturier   B. Protestantisme: 15846R.

   66 ff. numbered recto only, plus 6 ff. not numbered. The "debat... touchant la conversion" is included, although not mentioned on the title page.

86. 1620 *Les Disputes,* etc.

   Troyes   Nicolas Oudot   Picot, Fichier

87. no date *Les Disputes,* etc.

   Paris   Pierre Menier   Brunet
                                            B. Protestantisme: 311

80 ff. numbered recto only, plus 8 ff. not numbered. Although not mentioned on the title page, the *débat* is again included on the unnumbered ff., under the complete title "Les grands debats, divisions et noises d'entre Jean Calvin et Theodore de Baise, touchant la conversion d'une damoiselle estant à l'article de la mort, et des disputes de Guillot le Porcher et de la Bergere contre ledict Calvin."

XVII

88. 1560 *Le Contrepoison des cinquante deux Chansons de Clement Marot, faulsement intitulées par luy Psalmes de David, faict et composé de plusieurs bonnes doctrines et sentences preservatives d'Heresie, tant pour les sains, que pour les malades et debilitez en la Foy de nostre mere saincte Eglise.*

    Paris　　　Pierre Gaultier　　　Brunet
    　　　　　　　　　　　　　　　Arsenal: 8°T. 934

    80 ff. numbered recto only. Dedicated to "treshault, trespuissant et magnanime Seigneur, Monseigneur le Prince de Piedmont Duc de Savoye." The last page contains a second dedication, including a short poem, to "Monsieur de Varmond, Maistre de la Chappelle du plain chant du Roy, Aulmonier ordinaire de la Royne mere, et abbé de Vallette." This is a major work, both for the number of its editions, and for the controversy it aroused. In the following year, appeared a refutation entitled *Singulier antidote contre le poison des chansons d'Artus Désiré, auxquelles il a damnablement et execrablement abusé d'aucuns psalmes du prophète royal David, fait par J. D. D. C.* The identity of the author has remained unknown.

89. 1560 *Contrepoison des 52 chansons de Cl. Marot*, etc.

    Rouen　　　Jean Oreval　　　Brunet

90. 1561 *Contrepoison*, etc... *Plus adjousté de nouveau certains lieux et passages des œuvres dudict Marot, par lesquelz l'on cognoistra l'Heresie et erreur d'iceluy.*

    Paris   Pierer Gaultier   Arsenal: 8°T. 935

    80 ff. numbered recto only. Same dedication as No. 88 above. The text has been slightly compressed to make room for documentary evidence against the opinions of Marot. The second dedication and little poem to M. de Varmond are missing from this edition.

91. 1561 *Contrepoison*, etc.

    Avignon   Loys Barrier   Picot: *Catalogue de la Collection Rothschild*: V.No. 3204

    80 ff. numbered recto only. Follows the 1560 edition of Paris.

92. 1562 *Contrepoison*, etc.

    Paris   Pierre Gaultier   Brunet
                                                   B. Nationale: Rés.A. 6168

    80 ff. numbered recto only. Reproduces the 1561 edition of Paris.

93. 1562 *Contrepoison*, etc.

    Avignon   Pierre Roux   Brunet
                                                   Br. Museum: 11474. a. 11

    78 ff.

94. 1562 *Contrepoison*, etc.

    Lyon   Michel Jove   Versailles: Goujet in-24° 61

95. 1567 *Contrepoison*, etc.

    Paris   Jehan Ruelle   B. Nationale: Rés. Ye.1865

    88 ff. numbered recto only. Very small. Text follows the 1561 edition of Paris.

XVIII.

96. 1560 *Grande source et fontaine de tous les maux*, etc.

    Paris   (no publisher given) Picot, Fichier

97. 1561 *La grande source et fontaine de tous maux procedente de la bouche des blasphemateurs du saint nom de Dieu. Avec l'ingratitude des mauvais riches envers les pauvres, et de la perdition des enfants par l'incorrection des peres et meres.*

    Paris   (no publisher given) Goujet
                                        Cioranesco

There is marked similarity between the titles of the various parts of this volume, which I have not been able to examine, and those of No. VII above, *Instruction crestienne* of 1553, opening the possibility that the earlier text has been reissued under a slightly modified title. There are several examples of such reeditions in the works of Désiré; see the bibliographical note at the end of this chapter. Lacking firm proof, however, I have preferred to list this title as a separate work.

XIX.

98. no date *Le grand Chemin celeste de la Maison de Dieu.*

    Paris   Thibault Bessault   Brunet

Brunet and Cioranesco guessed that this edition appeared quite early in Désiré's career. Lacking a firm date, however, I have placed it with the 1565 edition, despite Brunet's note: "antérieur de quelques années" to the edition of 1565.

99. 1565 *Le grand Chemin celeste de la Maison de Dieu pour tous vrays Pelerins Celestes, traversans les desertz de ce monde, et des choses necessaires et requises pour parvenir au port de Salut, par M. Artus Désiré.*

    Paris   Thibault Bessault   Brunet
                                                Mazarine: 37-210 (2e partie)

40 ff. not numbered. Dedicated to "treshaulte, tresnoble, et trespuissante Dame, Madame la Duchesse de Parme, gouvernante es pais de Flandres et Artois." It consists solely of 8-syllable quatrains, ABAB.

100. 1575 *Le moyen de voyager seurement par les champs, sans estre destroussez des larrons et volleurs, et le chemin que doibvent tenir les voyagiers, Pelerins et Marchans.*

    Paris   Anthoine Hoüic   Brunet
                                                Arsenal: 8°BL 15.309

40 ff. not numbered. Dedicated to "treshaulte et puissante Dame, Madame Diane, de France, mareschalle de Montmorency, Duchesse de Chasteleraut." In the words of Brunet: "Ce petit poème... est non seulement le même ouvrage, mais aussi la même édition que celui qui porte pour titre: *Le grand chemin celeste,* etc... (1565): on en a simplement changé le titre, en substituant une dédicace (à la Maréchale de Montmorency) à celle qui était adressée à la duchesse de Parme."

XX.

101. 1568 *Secret Conseil sur la refformation des abuz de ce royaume fait par Mess. Artus Désiré Prestre: au nom des Caillettes Catholicques Badaux de Paris addressé au Roy Charles ix, 1568.*

    Unpublished.

    B. Nationale: Manuscript Collection
Rasse des Noeux
BN Ms Fr 22.561
ff. 58v-67v.

19 manuscript pages. For the most part 8-syllable quatrains, ABAB. The text is given in full in a later chapter. The chief elements of Désiré's advice are to retire the Queen Mother from active political affairs, reform abuses in clerical and judicial appointments, wipe out all the heretics in France.

XXI.

102. 1571 *L'origine et source de tous les maux de ce monde, par l'incorrection des peres et meres envers leurs enfans, et de l'inobedience d'iceux, Ensemble de la trop grande familiarité et liberté donnée aux servans et servantes, Avec un petit discours de la visitation de Dieu envers son peuple Chrestien par afflictions de guerre, peste et famine. Par M. Artus Désiré.*

    Paris   Jean Dallier   Goujet
B. Nationale: R. 18274

50 ff. numbered recto only.

103. 1571 *L'origine et source de tous les maux*, etc.

    Paris   Jean Dallier   B. Nationale: Rz. 3359

    50 ff. numbered recto only. Apparently identical with the preceding entry for 48 ff., but showing differences in lineation of last 2 ff.

104. 1573 *L'origine et source de tous les maux*, etc.

    Lyon   Michel Jove   Brunet

    At end: "A Lyon, imprimé par Pierre Roussin, Baudrier, II, 132."

XXII.

105. 1574 *Le desordre et scandale de France, par les Estats masquez et corrompus, contenant l'eternité des peines deües pour les pechez, et de la retribution des Eleuz et predestinez de Dieu. Composé par M. Artus Desiré.*

    Paris   Guillaume Jullien   Versailles: Rés. C. 264
    Rouen: 3976

    40 ff. numbered recto only. Dedicated to "treshaulte et puissante dame, Madame Diane de France Marechale de Montmorenci, Duchesse de Chasteleraut." The whole work is composed in alexandrines, ABAB.

106. 1575 *Le desordre et scandale de France*, etc.

    Paris   (no publisher given) Cioranesco

107. 1577 *Le desordre et scandale de France*, etc.

    Paris   Guillaume Jullien   Brunet
    Gachet d'Artigny

    32 ff.

XXIII.

108. 1574 *La singerie des Huguenots, marmots et guenons de la nouvelle derrision Theodobeszienne: contenant leur arrest et sentence par jugement de raison naturelle. Composé par M. Artus Desiré.*

Paris   Guillaume Jullien   Brunet
Ste Geneviève
B. Protestantisme:
(André) 723

8 ff. not numbered, plus 40 ff. numbered recto only. Dedicated to "treschrestien Roy de France Charles Neufiesme." There is a preliminary poem, printed as 6-syllable lines rhyming only on the even-numbered lines: thus alexandrines. This is followed by a long prose section, then at folio 26v another poem in 10-line stanzas of 8-syllable lines, then a final exhortation in prose. This work seems to be today the most widely distributed of all Désiré's works. There are copies at Geneva, British Museum, Versailles, Bibliothèque du Protestantisme, and incomplete copies at the Bibliothèque Nationale and the Arsenal.

109. 1856 *La singerie des Huguenots*, etc.

Reprinted in Montaiglon, *Recueil de poésies françoises*, IV, pp. 24-30 (1856). This reprint contains only the preliminary poems, 8 ff. not numbered in the 1574 edition. It was perhaps republished from the copy in the Bibliothèque Nationale, which contains only this same preliminary material.

XXIV.

110. 1578 *Le ravage et deluge des chevaux de louage, contenant la fin et consommation de leur miserable vie.*

Avec le Retour de Guillot le Porcher, sur les miseres et calamitez de ce regne present.

Paris   Guillaume Jullien   Brunet
B. Nationale: Rés.
Ye.1742 & 3
Arsenal: 8°BL 10.841

55 ff. numbered recto only. There are really two separate works: *Ravage et deluge,* mostly prose, and *Retour de Guillot,* mostly verse.

111. 1581 *Le ravage et deluge,* etc.

(no place given)   (no publisher given)   Picot, Fichier

XXV.

112. 1587 *Les Quinzes Signes advenuz ès parties d'Occident* Published by William Heist, *Studies in the Romance Languages and Literatures,* #72 ("Sermon Joyeux" and "Polemic").

Artus Désiré showed as much originality in his invention of titles as in any other aspect of his work. Despite the array of different titles, there is a great deal of repetition of the same material in his various works. In several cases, in fact, the same, or almost the same, text appeared under two, and at least once, three different titles.

The following is a partial list of his double titles:

1. *Miroir* (1547)   — *Deffensoire* (1547): an expanded version.
2. *Combatz* (1550) — *Batailles et victoires* (1553): same text.
3. *Loyauté* (1550) — *Grans abus* (1578): presumably same text.
4. *Grand chemin* — *Moyen de voyager* (1575): same text and edition.

5. *Hymnes ecclésiastiques* (1553) — *Hymnes en françois* (1561): same text.
   Plaisans et armonieux cantiques (1561): same text.
6. *Grandes chroniques* (1558) — *Regretz... d'une demoiselle* (1558) extract.
7. *Instruction* (1553) — *Grande source* (1561): presumably same text.
8. In addition, there are numerous instances of borrowing from his own published and unpublished works:

   a) *Deffensoire* (1550 epistre) — *Hymnes* (1561 prose) — much of the same text.

   b) *Secret conseil* (1568 unpubl.) — *Singerie* (1574) — heavy borrowing.

Another curious point (on which it would probably be unwise to insist) is that when he altered his titles, he often did so in a manner to take advantage of a changed climate of opinion or an altered situation in the nation. Thus the title *Instruction chrestienne*, which bespoke a naïve and perhaps unchallenged piety in 1553, seems to have become in 1561 *Grande source et fontaine de tous les maux*, indicating that certain assumptions about a unified and Catholic France could no longer be taken for granted. Similarly, the *Grand chemin celeste* of an early date, reappeared in 1575 as the *Moyen de voyager seurement par les champs*; again it seems probable that in 1575 a reference to the difficulties of travel in France, a direct result of the religious wars, was a better literary enticement than a banal "pilgrim's progress." The age of innocence and Pierre Doré had given way to a more militant intolerance.

Chapter III

BRIEF ANALYSIS OF THE WORKS OF ARTUS DÉSIRÉ

Introduction

The importance of Artus Désiré's works is not of a literary order. Nor was it his main purpose to make a literary reputation for himself. His primary interest was in theology, and in the preservation of the French public from what he considered the poison of Protestant heresy. In an age when poetry was an accepted medium of expression for any subject, he chose to produce his propaganda in verse form. This was insufficient to make of him a poet; but he himself would have measured his success less by his poetic reputation than by the impact of his ideas. Even those few admirers he has found through the centuries apologize for the deficiencies of his poetic invention, and limit their praise to the soundness of his understanding of the Catholic viewpoint. Niceron had dismissed him as a muddled clown: "Comme la science et la capacité lui manquoient, il tâchoit d'y suppléer par des bouffonneries et des plaisanteries."[1] But abbé Goujet, while scarcely approving his "buffoonery," nevertheless saw in him a soundly based orthodox thinker: "... on y voit en général plus de turlupinades que de raisonnements, plus d'injures que de preuves, plus de bouffonneries que de sérieux et de gravité, plus de verbiage que de solidité.... Je ne dirai pas cependant avec le Père Niceron qu'il manquoit de science et de capacité. On voit par ses

---

[1] Niceron, XXXV, 284.

écrits qu'il avoit lu avec soin les livres saints, qu'il étoit au fait des points controversés, et qu'il n'ignoroit ni les objections des nouveaux hérétiques, ni les réponses péremptoires qui les renversent..." ²

In this century, his only admirer, F. Charbonnier, did not venture to defend either his fanaticism or his style; but he too found that Désiré was thoroughly aware of the theological points in controversy, and gave clear voice to the orthodox position. ³

Those bibliophiles who have taken note of editions of his works, claim to do so only because of their rarity; intrinsically they are devoid of interest. In the words of Niceron, Désiré "n'est connu que par un grand nombre de mauvais ouvrages, qui ne sont recherchés des curieux qu'à cause de leur rareté." ⁴

In his study of militant literature in the 16th century, Charles Lenient begrudgingly devoted a few pages to Artus Désiré's pamphlets. Not that he was impressed by their style or content, but he saw in Désiré one of the first articulate Catholic voices to be raised in French against the heretics. ⁵

Apart from this meager treatment Artus Désiré has been neglected, except by a few scholars who have taken note of one or another of his separate works, usually in connection with something else. ⁶ This neglect is clearly justified from the literary standpoint. But despite his intellectual and artistic limitations, the fanaticism and violence of his pamphlets played some role in mobilizing opinion against the Protestants. From this point of view alone, his career deserves to be better known.

---

² Goujet, XIII, 132-3.
³ Charbonnier, F., *La poésie française et les guerres de religion*, p. 5; "En dehors des injures grossières auxquelles on est bien contraint de s'habituer quand on lit de pareilles oeuvres, certains points dogmatiques ou moraux sont clairement exposés." And page 358: "Il insiste tout particulièrement, dès les premières pages, sur cet esprit de tradition que les protestants se refusent à reconnaître comme nécessaire au christianisme.... Il n'est pas moins incisif quand il parle de la foi sans les oeuvres."
⁴ Niceron, loc. cit.
⁵ Lenient, pp. 221-4.
⁶ Thus, some of his anti-Marot statements have been gathered by C. A. Mayer in his study of *La religion de Marot*; certain aspects of his career, and the question of authorship of the *Passevent parisien*, were discussed by H. Shaw, in her critical edition of *Le pape malade*; and A. Carter treated his *Grandes chroniques et annales* in a lengthy article.

Noel Béda, symbol of the persecutions of the early 16th century, had died in 1537. The *Ligue*, formed to complete the work begun by Béda and continued by a host of lesser figures from the Sorbonne and the Parlement, was not formed until almost forty years later. But in the interim two developments should be noted: the battlefield had shifted from the Sorbonne to the street; and the language of controversy had changed from Latin to French. If the ignorance and violence of Béda are almost exactly reechoed by the preachers of the *Ligue*, it was in no small part the result of Désiré's indefatigable pamphleteering, which filled most of the intervening years.

Reference notes accompanying quotations from the various texts will indicate the order number of the edition used based on the numbering system of Chapter II, plus the page number, if any, or, lacking the page number, the appropriate folio number: for example "(#26, p. 213)" or "(#78, f.º A8 verso)."

1. Theological Controversy

II. *Miroer-Deffensoire*

The *Miroer des francs Taupins* and its expanded version the *Deffensoire de la foy chrestienne* constitute the first major work by Artus Désiré. The Miroer is a fairly long discussion, in 10-syllable couplets, of the major points in controversy between catholics and protestants. There are no formal subdivisions, and the progression of ideas is not always clear. Nonetheless there is a certain logic to its development. Approximately the first half is devoted to an elucidation of theological points, which are strung one after the other in a hit-or-miss fashion, liberally interspersed with the grossest insults towards "Luther," and those "Luthériens" who do not accept the orthodox catholic view of such things as veneration of the saints and relics, transubstantiation, and purgatory. The remainder of the work consists of a very harsh criticism of clerical abuses, especially plurality of benefices and moral laxity, together with a stinging satire of certain "femmes theologiennes," who without training deem themselves competent to take issue with more than one thousand years of truth transmitted by the Church. The discussion is thus in part theological and in part social. The same two elements recur in almost all of his subsequent works.

Goujet pronounced his theological opinions sound, but gave no praise for his presentation, even adding that "la défense de l'Eglise étoit assés mal entre les mains d'un pareil écrivain." In fact, although his opinions may have been orthodox, his arguments took the form of repetition of the opinion more often than an explanation of it. Perhaps for this reason he frequently fell back upon violent vituperation: How do we know that God approved veneration of the saints? To think otherwise would do God an injustice, for

> Lutheriens, malheureux reprouvez,
> Imposez-vous en vostre orde heresie
> Au Dieu vivant peché de jalousie...?
>
> (#3, f°. A7 recto)

And directly against Luther:

> O production d'infernalle vermine,
> Maistre cruel et rage tyrannique,
> Ne suffit-il à ta main plutonique
> Avoir descrit actes injurieuses
> Contre les sainctz, et vierges glorieuses,
> Sans debeller le sainct verbe divin ...?
> (#3, f°. Bii verso)

Occasionally he reached even more eloquent levels of invective:

> Je vous demande, entre vous idiotz
> Qu'on deust brusler à beaux fagots de paille....
> (#8, f°. Bii verso)

and

> Gens malheureux, pleins d'incredulité,
> Martyrs d'enfer, plongez en puante huyle....
> (#8, f°. Bii verso)

Perhaps the matter of theology lends itself only with difficulty to artistic treatment; in any case, Artus Désiré is somewhat more successful in his description of the social evils of "le temps qui court." The full impact of his social doctrine will become apparent in the course of this study; but a few lines, not without eloquence because they state simply a nostalgia for the "good old days" of an earlier generation, give a hint of his conservatism:

> Ilz ont basty, et nous debatissons,
> Dieu ont cogneu, nous le descongnoissons,
> Dieu ilz ont craint, sans fin nous l'offensons,
> Bien ont vescu, apres eux nous mourons,
> Ilz ont chanté, maintenant nous plorons,
> Nous plorons, quoy? la couple rigoureuse
> De nostre vie, avare et malheureuse,
> Qui nous conduit au feu abominable....
> (#3, f°. E8 recto)

Whenever he approached social questions, he was prone to place a heavy responsibility for the ills of the world upon the hapless shoulders of women. In matters of fostering heresy, he held women more guilty than men:

> Congnoissiez-vous ma dame et sa grand fille
> Celle qui porte un nouveau testament,
> Ouy, dit l'autre, et à mon jugement
> Je la congnois. N'est-ce pas l'amoureuse
> Qui tant se farde, un petit glorieuse,
> Demy bourgeoise et demy damoiselle,
> Qui tousjours porte un livre sous l'esselle
> ... ...
> Elle entend bien. Et quoy: la verité.
> Elle triomphe en la theologie....
> ... ...
> Je vous demande, amys, est-ce pour rire,
> Est-ce pour bien soy resjouir a l'ame
> De veoir porter soubz les bras de ma dame
> De ce Luther la nouvelle alliance,
> Qui par orgueil et damnable ignorance
> Pensent scavoir plus que n'a faict sainct Pierre?
> Quand sont ensemble, et ont le cul à terre,
> L'une viendra contre l'honneur de Dieu
> Prendre au rebours le livre sainct Matthieu.
> L'autre dira, ma commerce et amye,
> Pardonnez-moy, je ne vous demens mye,
> Mais au regard de ce propos icy
> Monsieur sanct Luc et sainct Marc dit ainsi....
> ... ...
> Si aujourdhuy quelque docteur allegue
> Un bon propos de la sainct escripture,
> Il sortira d'infernalle closture
> Une ydiotte, une sotte, une infame,
> Qui jurera, par la foy de mon ame
> Il a failly au quatriesme chapitre:
> Car sainct Marc dit en sa premiere epistre
> Tout le contraire, ha, le meschant cagot.
>   (#3, f°. Cii recto-Cv recto)

For their primary responsibility in propagating the new ideas, Désiré spelled out the punishments to which such women should be subjected:

> Helas! mon Dieu, que n'ay-je le fagot,
> Et le flambeau, pour brusler cest ordure.
> O adultere, orde progeniture,

> Las, est-ce à toy d'alleguer les chapitres
> De l'evangile, et de lire aux epistres
> Mises en prose ou en rithme Françoise.
> Au temps qui court ma dame la bourgeoise
> Me respondra: Si mon pere et ma mere
> Y ont erré pas ne veux ainsi faire,
> De mon salut je seray curieuse.
>   Au feu, au feu, bruslez la malheureuse,
> Bruslez cela, que jamais on n'en parle.
> Veu qu'elles sont atteintes du scandale,
> Et qu'à l'erreur on les voit condescendre,
> Ne doit-on pas de leurs corps faire cendre,
> Sans les pugnir par amende honnorable.
> Ceste sentence envers Dieu n'est louable,
> Ceste sentence est pleine d'injustice,
> Depuis quell'sont reprinses de ce vice
> La mort s'ensuyt, ou bien on leur fait tort....
>
>   (#3, f°. Ciii recto)

Equally as important in the scale of social abuses, to judge from the space allotted to it, is the laxity prevalent in monastic orders, and the clergy generally. Operating as he does at a low social level, he has no doubt as to the reason for this laxity: it is that the important positions go to the noble families, in order that their younger sons be provided with adequate income. The results are lack of vocation among the prelates, and lack of discipline in the rank and file:

> Or sur ce point un mot je vous demande:
> Qui est la cause, et la clé principalle,
> Que ce jourdhuy abusion claustralle
> Regne et domine en voz infames cueurs?
> C'est pour raison qu'estes trop gros seigneurs
> Et au moyen de voz grands benefices:
> Car de l'argent de voz riches offices
> Entretenez une vie orde et sale,
> Si tresmondaine et pleine de scandalle:
> Que tout le peuple en est scandalizé,
> Et vostre etat tant vil et desguisé,
> Qu'on vous en porte une mortelle hayne.
>   Est-ce l'estat, est-ce le train d'un moyne,
> Aller, venir, soy pourmener par ville,
> Dire bon jour, Dieu gard la belle fille,
> Comme vous va? Ha! moynes renyez,
> Moynes claustriers, gens excommuniez,

Craignez-vous point que Dieu ne vous confonde?
N'avez-vous pas tous renoncé le monde,
Et faict le veu de vivre en pauvreté?
Besoing seroit, et de necessité
Que vous n'eussiez en maniment deniers,
Et qu'on vous tint comme gens prisonniers,
Dessouz les clefz, sans sortir hors du cloistre.
Vous n'estes pas comme vous deussiez estre,
De vos pechez le monde est estonné.
... ...
La pauvre eglise est deserte et destruicte,
Comme j'ay dict, veufve elle est sans conduite,
En pleurs et plains se complaint du pasteur,
Qui de ses biens est grand dissipateur,
Et passe temps à jouer des hautz-boys,
Gros chiens nourrit, le pauvre est aux aboys
Qui ploure et crie, et de froid resue, nu,
Ce temps pendant que du gros revenu
Monsieur l'abbé se fait frotter l'eschine
Au pres du feu, qui murmure et rechigne
Comme un pourceau, gros et gras, mis en mue.
 De cest abus le cueur et sang me mue,
De cest abus je m'esbahis que Dieu
Ne les confond, tant l'abbé que le lieu,
Veu qu'il n'y a justice ne raison
Qu'un simple enfant d'une pauvre maison,
Sage et discret n'y puisse estre receu.
Jamais, jamais, s'il n'est de lieu yssu,
Ou ayt faveur par compare ou commere,
De par l'abbé ne tenu frere (sic)
C'est tout abus, et ne s'y fault attendre:
Povres enfants nous ne voyons point rendre
Ne recevoir à telle dignité.
 D'où vient cela faute de charité
Faute de bien, et qu'il n'a pas de quoy.
Communément à present voyez-moy
Ces gros seigneurs, riches et triumphans,
S'ilz ont un, deux, trois, quatre, cinq enfans,
Aux trois feront le froc d'abus porter
De paour qu'ils ont de leur desheriter
Des biens terriens, abusiz et damnables.
 Dont puis apres les courages muables
De ces moyneaux, sentent le feu d'enfer
Tant qu'ilz sont pires que Lucifer,
Et plus mondains que paillards du bordeau:
L'un pigne, l'autre fait le beaubeau,

> Portant le chaulce et braye decouppée
> Pour demonstrer qu'il est homme d'espée,
> Né et nourry, extrait de noble race:
> Jure "mort dieu," et "sang dieu" par menace,
> Tout veult tenir en sa subjection.
> Ne voylà pas belle profession?
> Ne voylà pas beau present faict à Dieu
> D'un sathanas, qui soubz l'umbre du lieu
> Dont est sorty, veult user de main forte,
> De nuict courir, vestu d'estrange sorte
> Comme un galland et bragard compagnon
> Portant par ville un petit froc mignon,
> Troucé, noué, au bras des braceletz,
> Des anneaux d'or, des poux? Fy! qu'ils sont laidz;
> Fy! qu'ilz sont ord, et à Dieu detestables,
> Gens desreiglez, moynes irraisonnables,
> Trop corrumpez le veu de pauvreté,
> Bien mieux vaudroit que la grand liberté
> Que vous avez fust fondue en abisme;
> S'il y avoit au cloistre bon regime
> Tout yroit mieux selon ma fantaisie....
>
> (#3, f°. Fii recto-Fiv recto)

Several editions of this work justify the title *Miroer des francs Taupins, autrement nommez Lutheriens,* etc. by appending a sort of separate little diatribe against the "francs Taulpins," which, with a "Ballade sur le temps qui court," occupies the last three folios. But in a more general way, the title is justified by Désiré's method, which was to first set down the heretical opinion which he intended to combat. This was the *Miroer*.

* * *

The *Deffensoire de la foy chrestienne, contenant en soy le Miroer des francs Taupins* is neither exactly the same work under a new name (there are several examples of this in Désiré's published works; see bibliographical note, chap. II), nor the older work combined with a new one (which the title suggests), nor an entirely new work. It is rather a reorganization and expansion of the *Miroer,* containing all the lines of the early text, and about as many more new ones.

The *Deffensoire* shows signs of a literary preoccupation which is largely lacking from the *Miroer.* It is divided into 18 distinct chapters, each accompanied by a "huitain," "dizain," or "onzain," summarizing the chapter, and breaking the monotony. In addition, certain material which had been scattered in the *Miroer* was gathered here to form more homogeneous divisions. Finally there are efforts at "poetic" composition in the most stilted manner, for example the opening lines which are a play on the surname of the author:

> Jay desiré, et tant plus je desire,
> Plus grand desir j'ay de corrompre l'ire,
> Et la fureur d'un tas de murmurans
> Contre la Foy, jour et nuict desirans
> Vivre en erreur et d'un desir ireux,
> Tendent aux fins d'un faux coeur desireuz....
> (#9, f°. Avi recto)

The chapter headings, in each of which the author defends the orthodox point of view, are as follows:

	ii	des images de saincte Eglise
	iii	de la priere des sainctz
	iv	de la vierge Marie
	v	de la veneration des Reliques
	vi	des chandelles et oblations
	vii	de l'eau beniste
	viii	du feu de Purgatoire
	ix	de la jeusne et institution du Caresme
	x	de la confession
	xi	du sainct Sacrement de l'autel
	xii	du Christ sans nommer Jesus
	xiii	des œuvres et merites
	xiv	du franc et libre arbitre
	xv	des pasteurs et prelatz de l'Eglise
	xvi	des pardons et indulgences
	xvii	de l'estat de Religion
	xviii	des femmes theologiennes
	—	Ballade sur le temps qui court

These subjects, to which he will return repeatedly in his subsequent writings, constitute a list of most of the theological points at issue between the two religions.

One of his favorite arguments for the truth of the catholic religion, an argument which makes its way into almost every one of his discussions, is the authority of tradition: Would God have allowed us to continue in error for all these centuries? It is the critical factor when he deals with the question of the "images des saints" in chapter two. After describing a Council at which:

>   ....fut dict et de tous soustenu,
>   Que c'estoit chose honnorable et requise
>   De les avoir en nostre mere eglise,
>   Pour la memoire et introduction
>   Du commun peuple, ayant devotion
>   Aux benoistz sainctz de la cour souveraine....
>
> (#9, f°. B verso)

he suggests:

>   Or regardez combien il y a d'ans,
>   Et assavoir si Dieu auroit permis
>   A noz parens et anciens amys,
>   Depuis ce temps avoir idolatré.
>   Et s'il n'auroit jusqu'au jourdhuy monstré
>   Le droit chemin de l'eternel repos.
>
> (#9, f°. B verso)

The chapter ends with an "Unzain":

>   Puisque le Sainct Esprit preside
>   Aux saincts conciles, il faut croire
>   Que tous les poinctz qu'on y decide,
>   Sont au profit du commun gerre,
>   Et qui n'y croit, grandement erre.
>   Dont croyons ce qui est escript,
>   Car rien ne vaut crier Christ! Christ!
>   A celuy qui les sainctz mesprise.
>   Les bons docteurs n'ont point rescript
>   D'eulx-mesmes sans le sainct esprit
>   Les ordonnances de l'eglise.
>
> (#9, f°. Bv verso)

and a "Sizain":

>   En despit de tous hereticques,
>   Les bons Chrestiens evangelicques

Auront representation
Des sainctz et ordres angelicques.
Par les images catholicques.
Car c'est de Dieu l'intention.
                    (#9, f°. Bv verso-Bvi recto)

The development of the argument in this sequence is typical of his method. Beginning with a statement of faith in the *Conciles,* he moves on to the argument that God would not have let us live in ignorance all these years. Good Christians will have images of the saints in their churches, because the *Conciles* are divinely inspired, and besides it is God's will.

In chapter four he reverts to the same authority to defend the Catholic adoration of the Virgin:

Est-il besoing faire un nouveau concile:
Est-il besoing laisser l'oppinion
De tous les sainctz, qui par bonne union
Ont discuté tout probleme doutable?
... ...
Ha, perversante orde langue vulpine,
Qui tant mesdictz de la digne pucelle,
Celle qui tous sainctz et sainctes precelle,
Dy-moi à qui nous porterons l'honneur,
Sinon à elle apres nostre Seigneur?
                    (#9, f°. Cii recto)

As usual the authority of tradition is buttressed by vilification.

In chapter five, "De la veneration des reliques," he again appeals to the comforting common sense of a long-established practice:

Entendez donc, mes freres et amys,
Que si c'estoit abusion et faincte,
De venerer le corps d'un sainct ou saincte,
Dieu n'auroit point si longtemps enduré
Que le deffault eust jusqu'icy duré....
                    (#8, f°. C4 verso)

In chapter six, "Des chandelles et oblations," his vituperation is accompanied by a willful misinterpretation of motive:

Ha, meschans gens, espritz malicieux,
Desraisonnez, qui demandez à tous,

> Que sert cela? plus gens de bien que vous
> L'ont ordonné, mais vostre vile secte
> A liberté est si serve et subiecte,
> Que vous taschez totalement destruire
> La loy de Dieu par vostre faulx mesdire,
> Pour et à fin d'estre exempts de tout bien,
> Dont il appert que vous ne vallez rien....
>
> (#8, f°. C9 verso)

He returns again, in his chapter "Des œuvres et merites," to the accusation that the heretics are seeking to evade their responsibility to lead a good life:

> Gens obstinez, cauteleux en malice
> Estimez-vous parvenir en la gloire
> De Paradis sans oeuvre meritoire?
> Estimez-vous par orgueil terrien
> Estre sauvez, sans faire au monde bien?
> Nenny vrayment, mais j'entens bien pourquoy
> Vous desniez les oeuvres de la Foy,
> C'est pour raison que francs vous voulez estre
> De labourer, et de Dieu recongnoistre,
> Pour et à fin d'estre exempts de bien faire....
>
> (#8, f° H5 verso)

The Calvinist distinction between practicing virtue to purchase salvation, and living in virtue as a sign of predestined salvation, escaped him.

III. *Combatz*

The *Combatz* represent a second major theological assault on the heretics. Du Gort frères had taken over publication of the *Miroer-Deffensoire* in 1549, perhaps on expiration of the two-year privilege accorded Jehan André of Paris in 1547; they now serve as a link to the new work, which they were the first to publish. This book covers most of the same ground as the earlier one, but with certain changes in style and emphasis. Unlike the *Deffensoire*, which was an adaptation of the *Miroer*, this is a new work. The raw material of the *Miroer* has this time been completely rewritten. But the publishers took some of the woodcut illustrations from their edition of the *Deffensoire* and used them, together with some new illustrations, in the new work.

BRIEF ANALYSIS OF THE WORKS OF ARTUS DÉSIRÉ

As was the case with the *Miroer*, there are few internal divisions in this work. The entire text of the *Combatz*, in fact, runs without a break for several thousand lines. In order to overcome the difficulty of finding his way through this mass of material, the reader is guided in some of the editions by margin notes, which provide him with a list of subjects treated. There are 43 of these notes which can be logically subdivided into 23 "combats," corresponding roughly to chapters. These are as follows:

1) Premier combat des livres en vulgaire et comme la saincte escripture ne se doibt translater en ladite langue.
   Marot allegué des heretiques.
   Saint Gregoire nazianzene reprouve les livres en vulgaire.
   Des femmes qui veulent interpreter la saincte escripture.

2) Combat sus la puissance du pape et comme il peut mauldire et excommunier.
   Les heretiques semblables à Cam qui descouvrit la honteuse nature de son pere.
   Les heretiques n'ont autre moyen de decevoir les simples gens sinon que les prestres sont malvivans.
   Des reproches qu'on donne aux princes de plusieurs abuz qui se commettent dont ilz ne scavent rien.
   Plusieurs pechez sont reservez au siege apostolique.

3) Combat sus les indulgences. Et comme le sainct pere a puissance de pardonner et remettre les pechez.
   Tout pape est dit pierre.

4) Combat sus la sentence de excommunication.
   La sentence du pasteur est grandement à craindre.
   Du concile de Bitunie où aucuns heretiques nyoient la puissance du pape et au meillieu de tout le peuple le sainct esprit descendit visiblement.
   Il est necessaire qu'en l'eglise il y ait un pasteur, autrement seroit la confusion de Babilone.

5) Combat de la puissance de l'eglise.

6) Combat sus la puissance des conciles, comme nous devons tous obeir à la determination d'iceux.

Tous princes doivent estre contrainz de assister aux conciles sur peine de privation de leurs royaumes.

7) Combat sus la pluralité des benefices.
En la diette de Paris faicte l'an mil deux centz trente, maistre Guillaume, chancelier de ladite ville, s'opposa sus la refformation des benefices dont revele apres sa mort qu'il estoit damné.

8) Combat de la confession auriculaire, et comme il est de necessité de confesser noz pechez au prestre autrement ne nous seront point pardonnez ne remis.
De troys pechez les juifz se confessent au prestre verbalement, c'est assavoir de blaspheme, d'adultere et d'homicide.

9) Combat sus aucuns abus et comme nous devons tous obeissance à nos pasteurs nonobstant leur mauvaise vie.

10) Combat sus les barbes des gens d'eglise et comme à eux n'appartient de la porter longue.

11) Combat sus les Chantz de l'eglise et comme c'est une chose catholique et saincte qui incite les cueurs des hommes à devotion.
Vision de Saint Ignace qui vid les anges chanter à deux parties.

12) Combat sus les ceremonies de nostre mere saincte eglise.

13) Combat sus la benediction du pain benit.

14) Combat sus la benediction de l'eau et comme elle efface les pechez venielz.
De l'eau d'expiation qui figuroit l'eau beneite de la loy de Jesus Christ.

15) Combat sus le feu de purgatoire et sur la deprecation des trespassez.
De troys hommes mors qui resusciterent au concile de Bethleem.

16) Combat sus le jeusne et de l'abstinence de la chair tant de caresme que vendredy samedy, vigiles, et quatre temps.

Les gourmans et charnelz corrumpent les traditions de nostre mere eglise pour complaire à leur ventre.

17) Combat sus la veneration des images des sainctz et sainctes de paradis.

18) Combat sus la priere et veneration des sainctz.
Unze cens ans que la saincte letanie fut faicte par sainct Memer archevesque de Vienne.
Il y a troys adorations l'atrie, iperdulie, et dulie.

19) Combat sus les oblations des chandelles et autres offertoires.
Murmure des heretiques sus les oblations et offertoires.

20) Combat sus la veneration des reliques des sainctz.

21) Combat sus le sainct sacrement de l'autel et comme la substance du pain et vin est transmuée au corps et sang de Jesus Christ.

22) Combat sus le liberal arbitre de l'homme.

23) Combat sus les oeuvres: Et de la justification de....

It is evident that this work embraces not only most of the topics covered by the Deffensoire, but also a number of others not previously touched upon, ranging from the trivial question of beards for priests, to the thorny controversy over papal authority.

The latter part of the volume, including in most editions more than 60 pages, is a vast allegory, in which the Church bemoans her lack of support and calls upon the faithful to defend her. The quality of these pages can be judged on the basis of a very few lines: here the faithful are marching to the defense of "nostre mere saincte Eglise:"

> Et vous, saint Pere, allez devant,
> Ainsi que feit le bon Urie,
> Et debandez l'artellerie.
> ... ...
> Et vous Cardinaulx, en bataille
> Manifestez vos grands vertus,
> Vous estes de rouge vestus.
> ... ...

> Sus, sus, à la guerre, à la guerre
> Evesques, Abbés, et Prelats
> Que faites-vous, estes-vous las,
> Quand il se fault mettre en defense?
> ... ...
> Dedans, dedans, allarme, allarme,
> Prieurs, curés, et simples Prestres,
> Marchez tous d'ordre après vos maistres.
> Et vous Messieurs les Reverends
> Docteurs, Bacheliers de Sorbonne,
> Que chacun de vous s'abandonne
> A comfuter ces Antechrists.
> Suyvez après Moynes, Moyneaux,
> Qui tenez de Saint Benoist l'ordre,
> Marchez sans faire aucun desordre.
> ... ...
> Au surplus vous enfants de Dieu,
> Nommez Chartreux, vivans en chartre,
> Vous estes fort bien pour combattre,
> Combien qu'on vous estime morts,
> Si estes-vous gens des plus forts
> Et des plus puissans de la terre,
> Pour bien combattre en cette guerre.
> (#27, f°. Aiiii et seq.)

Finally a section which invariably formed a part of the *Description*, despite its separate title, is called "les raisons pourquoy les Hereticques ont laissé la saincte cité de Dieu, et se sont armez contre elle." This is a recapitulation of the position of the Huguenots, with a much briefer refutation.

Despite the low literary level of the work, it does show evidence of several efforts on the part of Artus Désiré to enliven it and make it more readable than his earlier works. Whereas the *Miroer* was disorganized, and the *Deffensoire*, although orderly, a straight exposition of his arguments, the *Combatz-Batailles* has been recast as a dialogue between a pilgrim to Rome, and a pilgrim to Geneva. Naturally the pilgrim to Rome has the better of every "combat"; but two factors tend to weaken his side. First, in order to demolish the Protestant arguments, Désiré must allow the Geneva pilgrim to state them, and this he does, often with very telling effect, especially in those matters treating of the shortcomings of the Catholic clergy, from the pope down to the lowest monk. In the second place, the torrent of abuse which the Roman pilgrim heaps upon his adversary in lieu of reasoned argumentation, abuse which the Protestant accepts with true Christian patience, often shows the Catholic to disadvantage.

For example, in the course of a long argument on translations of the scriptures, *Antipapiste* advances a rather mild position:

> Je dy qu'ils sont aussi faciles
> A gens rustiques et champestres
> Comme aux plus clers et sçavantz prestres
> De ce bas et mortel repaire,
>   Christ dit-il pas que Dieu son pere
> Par sa clemence et charité
> A revelé la verité
> Aux petitz et caché aux grans.
>   (#19, f°. 14 verso)

To which *Papiste* responds with more vigor than logic:

> O entre vous maulditz errans
> Qui contentez voz appetis?
> Vous estimez-vous des petis?
>   Vous remplis d'orgueil et encombre
> Vous dictes-vous estre du nombre
> Des humbles et obeissans....
>   (#19, f°. 14 verso)

Again, after *Antipapiste* has deplored the injustice of papal indulgences, *Papiste* replies with even more heat and less *à propos*:

> Si ce n'estoit compassion
> Que j'ay de ton ame vollage
> L'auroys le cueur et le courage
> De t'estrangler de mes deux mains
> O faulx ennemy des Rommains
> Mauldict successeur de Jehan Hus....
>   (#19, f°. 26 recto.

When his other arguments fail him, *Papiste* can always, and frequently does, fall back on authority to silence his interlocutor; *Antipapiste* professes that:

> En tes propos rien je n'entens
> Et ne puis nullement comprendre

> Ou c'est qu'il peult trouver et prendre
> Tant de folz pardons qu'il vous donne
> Ne pourquoy c'est qu'il les ordonne
> Si ce n'est pour avoir argent
> Et pour tromper la pauvre gent
> Qui est facile à decevoir.
>
> (#19, f°. 32 verso)

The answer of *Papiste* is once again far from convincing:

> Ie te dis et te fais sçavoir
> Pour eviter faulx accidentz
> Qu'il fault en despit de tes dentz,
> Ou bien estre à jamais en peine,
> Croire qu'il a puissance pleine....
>
> (#19, f°. 32 verso)

In view of the cogency of *Antipapiste*'s arguments, the reader can almost forget at times that the author was one of the most fanatical opponents of the Calvinists, and that it was only by inadvertence that he gave his adversaries the better of the argument.

XVI. *Disputes de Guillot*

The *Disputes* are a major item in Désiré's attack on Calvin and Geneva specifically, as distinct from his continuous battle against the Protestant movement in general. The work is the third of his "major" theological treatises, major in the sense that they include a general attack on all fronts of the controversy, and reiterate the orthodox point of view on all important disputed issues.

As in the case of the *Deffensoire* and the *Combatz*, a list of chapter heading will give an accurate picture of the scope of his work:

1) Du Seigneur et du Christ.

2) De Guillot le Porcher qui va cercher ses pourceaux à Geneve.

3) De l'Eglise maligne de Martin Luther.

4) De la verité cachée aux grans, et revellée aux petis.

5) De l'incredulité et obstination des Heretiques.

BRIEF ANALYSIS OF THE WORKS OF ARTUS DÉSIRÉ

6) Du murmure des Heretiques sus la pluralité des Benefices.

7) Autre murmure des dispences mal impetrées de la court Romaine.

8) Du jeusne et institution de Kresme par la tradition des Apostres.

9) Du murmure contre l'abus et mauvais vie d'aucuns Prelatz.

10) De l'adoration des Images.

11) De la veneration et priere des saincts.

12) De la veneration des corps Saincts et Reliques.

13) Des offertoires et chandelles.

14) De l'institution du Pain benist.

15) Du feu du Purgatoire, et de la priere qu'on fait pour les Trespassez.

16) De l'institution et vertu de l'eau Beniste.

17) De la confession verballe que nous sommes tenus de faire aux prestres.

18) De la transsubstantiation du Pain et vin au corps et sang de nostre Sauveur Jesus Christ, au Sainct Sacrement de l'Autel.

19) De l'authorité et puissance du Pape et des Pardons et indulgences qu'il confere.

20) Des oeuvres et merites despendantes du liberal Arbitre.

21) La grande genealogie des Hereticques.

22) De l'abomination et ruyne procedante de leur doctrine.

It is clear from the headings that there is little in this book which he had not already thoroughly discussed in the earlier ones, but he does use a new device in presenting the arguments. It will be remembered that the *Deffensoire* consisted of straight exposition of Désiré's ideas, giving him the opportunity to develop his arguments without fear of interruption, but resulting in a text which was hopelessly dull. Perhaps to obviate this difficulty, and to render his views palatable to persons not already predisposed in their favor, he turned next, in the *Combatz,* to dialogue between a Catholic and a Protestant. We have already observed that, while enlivening the text to some degree, this method, by allowing the Protestant an almost equal opportunity to express his views, occasionally placed the Catholic at a disadvantage, thus defeating its own purpose.

In the *Disputes* he attempted to overcome the weakness of the second method without reverting to the first: we find here another dialogue, but not this time between equals. Instead, no less a personnage than Calvin himself debates with two simple, uneducated folk, "Guillot le Porcher" and the "Bergère de Saint Denis, en France."

As the Bergère is finishing her argument with Calvin over the terms "Seigneur" and "Christ," Guillot enters, looking for his "pourceaux" which, in a rather obvious allegory which is never developed further, he expects to find in Geneva. He is outspoken and often violent in his language. From the beginning the purpose is evidently to pit two little Catholic Davids against the Protestant Goliath, and thus capture the sympathy of the reader for the underdogs. When Calvin boasted that many rich and powerful people came to Geneva, the rejoinder was that true Christian charity was to be found more frequently among the poor:

> Quand il fault faire quelque bien
> Aux povres gens de ce qu'on a,
> Les plus petis le font tresbien,
> Mais Monsieur n'entend point cela.
>
> (#77, f° 17 recto)

This is in rather marked contrast to the alignment of classes in the *Combatz.* There the Protestant had championed the right of the little people to interpret Scripture for themselves, and the only rejoinder of the Catholic was "What! You consider yourselves little and humble, when you so clearly commit the sin of pride." This time Désiré had prepared his position in advance; by expressing his views through his peasants he is able to show the church of Rome as champion of the humble.

Not only do they overwhelm Calvin with insults and invectives, as their predecessor "pelerin romain" had done to his fellow pilgrim, for example "comme vous, anes imbeciles, qui niez la tradition," (#77, f°. 25 recto) but they also have the better of every argument, forcing the eminent theologian to admit defeat on each point before moving on to the next one. The typical argument develops as follows: after objecting to the use of candles in the Catholic service and listening patiently to the explanation offered by his interlocutors, Calvin retreats:

> Or je confesse notamment
> Que la coustume est treshonneste,
> D'en porter ordinairement
> Les jours de ferie et de feste,
> Et pource plus ne m'en enqueste
> Mais du pain benist seulement,
> Qui me tourmente tant la teste
> Que j'empers tout l'entendement....
> (#77, f°. 44 recto)

Again he listens to the Catholic position, then admits that:

> Sur voz raisons je me repose
> Car en ce m'avez satisfaict,
> Mais il y a une autre chose
> Qu'il me semble estre un grand forfaict,
> C'est de la priere qu'on faict
> Pour les deffunctz, par vos editz....
> (#77, f°. 44 recto)

And so forth, on each point, until in the end Calvin is forced to admit his complete defeat:

> Or suis-je le plus esperdu
> Que je fus onc en jour de vie,
> Car je voy bien que sui perdu
> Et damné par ma punaisie,
> Pour complaire à la fantaisie
> D'un tas de curieuses femmes
> J'ay faict mourir par Heresie
> Un million de povres ames....
> (#77, f°. 68 recto)

Yet he cannot recant, for

> .... que diroit tout le monde
> Si je reprenoys vostre Loy?
> Je mourroys de deuil et esmoy
> Si cela m'estoit reproché,
> Dont il fault en despit de moy
> Que je meure avec mon peché....
>
> (#77, f°. 69 recto)

Among so many arguments already used so many times before, there are three points which deserve special mention. The first is the violence of Calvin's denunciation of the way of life of the Catholic clergy. True, we have read all this before, but seldom in such scathing terms:

> Se sont de gros Asnes ignares
> Pleins de toutes concupiscence,
> Si ambitieux et avares
> Qu'ilz n'ont aucune conscience,
> Et si adonnez à offence
> Ainsi que chacun peut cognoistre,
> Que s'il se faict quelque insolence
> Il y a tousjours quelque prestre.
> Tousjours quelque prestre il y a
> Es lieux où se font les querelles,
> Et tout l'estat de ces gens là
> Est vacquer aux oeuvres charnelles,
> Et à nourrir des Macquerelles
> Qui ne font autre cas sinon,
> Leur mener de jeunes pucelles
> Et femmes de mauvais renom.
>
> (#77, f°. 21 recto)

To which Guillot replies in effect that all this is true, but we owe them obedience nonetheless:

> Je te respons quant à ce poinct
> Que nonobstant qu'ilz soient pecheurs,
> Que leurs pechéz n'empeschent point
> Qu'ilz ne soyent noz superieurs....
>
> (#77, f°. 21 recto)

The second point to note is the slanderous nature of some of the accusations against the Protestants. Artus Désiré had always dwelt on their "paillardise," but never before had he detailed such an accusation as this one from the Bergère, that:

>...dedans voz chambres infames
>Vous tenez bien une Venus,
>Et plusieurs figures de femmes
>Aupres de gros paillards tous nuds.
>Et donc si vous les avez painctes
>Pour vous exciter à luxure,
>Pourquoy n'aurons-nous la figure
>Aussi bien des Sainctz et des Sainctes?
>
>(#77, f°. 32 verso)

Finally we might take note of the violence and intemperance of the punishment which both the simple, Catholic peasants wish for all heretics:

>*Guillot*: Tous les jours par les bois je vois...
>   En criant aux juges Françoys
>   Pour Dieu, bruslez tous ces pourceaux....
>
>(#77, f°. 40 recto)

And the Bergère voices the same sentiments when she asserts that:

>C'est la maniere de parler
>De noz paillardeaux Hereticques
>Qu'on deust à petit feu brusler
>Pour leurs erreurs problematicques.
>
>(#77, f°. 52 verso)

The *débat d'entre ledict Calvin et Theodore de Baise, touchant la conversion d'une demoiselle...*, which is included in some, if not all, of the editions subsequent to 1560, is a version of the tale, originally part of the Grandes Chroniques (No. 73), concerning Mlle. Budee and her conversion. Here, as in the *Regretz, Complainctes et Lamentations* (No. 74), the name of the demoiselle is not given.

XV. *Articles*

The text of 53 quatrains is for the most part a diatribe against various sinners, first of all, the delinquent churchmen, for whom he recommends "reform." For various other categories of "sinner" he suggests the following punishments:

Sinners	*Punishments*
dishonest judges	unspecified
Lutherans	burn them
those who speak against saints	burn them
blasphemers	unspecified
children	spank and whip them
malicious	cut out their tongues
gamblers, card players	to the galleys
"vacabons"	unspecified "discipline"
frequenters of brothels, cabarets and gambling halls	execute them
pimps and madams	to the gallows
women	melt down their jewelry
usurers	unspecified
preachers of false doctrine	burn them
those of the "conventicules" and "conciliabules"	burn them
those possessing false books	burn them

All these and several other admonitions occur in the space of about two hundred lines, the general quality of which can be judged by the first and last stanzas:

> Qui vouldra la paix obtenir,
> Qu'on mette peine de punir
> Les pechez du peuple qui erre;
> Autrement tousjours aurons guerre.
> . . . .
> (#75, f°. 8 recto)

>   Reformons donc tous ces pointz-là
>   Pour le grand peril où nous sommes,
>   Et pour certain la paix sera
>   Criée entre Dieu et les hommes.
>
>   (#75, f°. 12 verso)

"or at least those who are left," it is a temptation to add.

XIX. *Grand Chemin*

This little work is an extensive allegory, a kind of pilgrim's progress, in the manner of Pierre Doré. Its quality can be gauged by the opening lines:

>   Tous pelerins et pelerines
>   Qui cerchez le chemin estroict
>   Des celestes maisons divines
>   Suyvez celuy qui va tout droict.
>   Pour aller au logis de Dieu
>   Fuyez le loup qui vous poursuit,
>   Et ne passez par autre lieu
>   Que par cestuy ce qui s'ensuit.
>   Premierement pour bien marcher
>   En ceste vie transitoire,
>   Ne vous chargez d'habit trop cher
>   Qui soit fourré de vaine gloire.
>   Pour vous gardez de l'insolence
>   Des eaux et vents, soyez vestus
>   D'un beau manteau de patience
>   Pasmenté de toutes vertus....
>
>   (quoted by Briquet *Bulletin du
>   Bibliophile,* 1855, pp. 503-4)

A few of the seventeen topics, in addition to the *manteau de patience,* which he developed at great length, are listed below, with an indication of the allegorical nature of the development.

1) Chapeau du pelerin celeste contre la concupiscence charnelle — (jeûne et abstinence)

2) L'hostellerie ou doibt loger le Pelerin celeste — (Eglise)

3) Les serviteurs et servantes de la dicte hostelerie — (anges et saints)

4) L'eau que le Pelerin doibt mettre en son vin — (larmes)

5) Le vin du Pelerin celeste — (sang de Jesus Christ).

VIII. *Desespoir testamentaire*

This pamphlet is cast in the form of a series of dialogues, but can scarcely be considered a dramatic work. It begins with a conversation between Luther (l'enfant de perdition) and the Church. He is severely chided for the schism he has created in the Christian world: although *Eglise* does not deny his claim that the wrong people obtain positions in the Church, she points out that it is not her fault, and that it does not justify disobedience:

> Crie donc dessus les abus
> Sans contredire à ma puissance,
> Car des abus qu'on faict en France
> Je ne suis cause nullement....
>
> (#53, f°. 156 verso)

The *enfant* persists in his argument, and threatens to use the current abuses as an excuse to found his own faith:

> Je prendray là mon fondement
> Pour abolir les sacrifices,
> Car je voy que les benefices
> Sont donnez à des gens incapables,
> Don se font maulx innumerables
> A raison de ceste avarice....
> . . . .
> Comme tous les diables d'enfer
> Pourroys-je prendre patience,
> De voir ceulx qui n'ont pas science
> Tenir les biens que deusse avoir?
> Je suis un homme de sçavoir,
> Docteur et prestre venerable,
> Trop plus suffisant et capable
> D'estre cardinal (bref et court)
> Qu'un tas de braves de la court....
>
> (#53, f°. 156 verso-157 recto)

BRIEF ANALYSIS OF THE WORKS OF ARTUS DÉSIRÉ 101

There we have Désiré's explanation for the defection of Luther: annoyance at not receiving cardinal's rank, an explanation repeated several times from the mouth of Luther himself.

At last the *enfant* is forced to accept excommunication from the Church, and we find him next pleading with God for mercy. But God is adamant: in reply to Luther's generous plea that the Calvinists in Geneva be shown the light God answers that they have only to listen to the Pope and the Church, he can do no more.

Finally, in debate with *Lucifer,* he is chided for his "paillardise," which had led him to damnation. Luther in despair then expresses the hope that if he must suffer, all other heretics will suffer with him; but even this thought affords him no comfort, for:

> S'ilz viennent en ce lieu damnable,
> Ma douleur en augmentera;
> Car leur peché m'accusera
> Devant Dieu, qui congnoist le faict....
> (#53, fº. 168 recto)

Then in a final burst of generosity he cries out:

> O povres mondains envieux,
> Si vous aviez la congnoissance
> De ce qui pend devant voz yeulx,
> Tant vous feriez grand penitence....
> (#53, fº. 168 verso)

"Profit by my miserable example," in other words, "and return to the church of Rome."

2. Polemics dealing with Geneva

X. *Passevent parisien*

In 1553 the French reading public was treated to a sparkling and cleverly executed satire, the *Epistola Magistri Benedicti Passavanti*, composed by Théodore de Bèze, but published anonymously. Although the Catholic-Protestant theological controversy had been raging for a number of years, this pamphlet introduced a new feature into the battle: it contrasted the serenely simple virtue of the Calvinists with the sodden vehemence and violence of the church leaders in Paris. According to the text, Pierre Lizet, premier président du Parlement de Paris, had sent his valet Passavant to Geneva to spy and report on the way of life he found there. Through his inept testimony in macaronic Latin, the Protestant leaders were exonerated from immorality and fanaticism, which sins were attributed instead to Lizet and his fellow Persecutors.

It was presumably the publication of this work which set off, between France and Geneva, a series of sharp exchanges, which continued until the outbreak of actual warfare turned all minds to other matters. These pamphlets no longer dealt exclusively with theological questions, but, like the prototype by de Bèze, contained a large element of slander on both sides.

The first counterattack from the Catholic side, in direct response to the *Passavanti*, was another pamphlet which appeared anonymously in 1556, entitled *Passevent parisien respondant à Pasquin romain de la vie de ceux qui sont allez demourer, et se disent vivre selon la reformation de l'Evangile, au païs jadis de Savoye: et maintenant soubz les Princes de Berne, et Seigneurs de Geneve: faict en forme de Dialogue*.

Although it attracted wide attention (at least seven separate editions in 1556 alone), it was not again reissued after that year until 1875, and must have quickly disappeared from view. As is evident from the title, it is an attempt to refute the work of de Bèze, while capitalizing on the other's title. From the standpoint of its composition it cannot compare with its model. Passevent is just returned from a stay in Geneva, where he has picked up a store of scandalous gossip, which he now passes on to his friend Pasquin. It is written in prose, and the interlocutors take a malicious pleasure in the recital of the philandering adventures of Calvin and his cohorts.

A few examples will serve to illustrate the spirit of the work. Passevent has related in detail to Pasquin the seduction of a nun by Calvin, her pregnancy, and the arrangements for her marriage to a "Chanoine," in order to conceal the fault of Calvin; all this gave rise to the following comments:

Pasquin: Et puis Calvin abandonna il ainsi sa truie pleine, sans revoir si le Chanoine y auroit rien affolé, ny gasté?

Passevent: Je vois bien que telz propos te plaisent, et je t'asseure qu'à eulx les faicts leur plaisent plus, jusques à ce qu'ilz en sont tous maigres blesmes et défaictz, tant que chacun de bon jugement diroit qu'ilz sortent de la fosse. Dont le pauvre menu peuple en est trompé et déçeu, pensant d'eux que ce soit par quelque austérité ou pénitence, laquelle ilz deffendent de faict, et de doctrine, niant toutes bonnes œuvres.... qui est la cause que Calvin et ses compaignons sont maintenuz d'un tas de bannis pour leurs crimes, ou bien d'un tas d'apostatz des Religions, pour vivre plus en leur liberté charnelle, et en tous vices, comme en récitant la vie d'un chacun je te diray. (#69, p. 8)

On the subject of the immorality which is alleged to exist in Geneva and other cities, they exchange the following remarks:

Pasquin: ...j'ay entendu dire qu'ilz endurent point de bourdeaux ni autres vices sans correction, ou punition, et pource ils veulent que chacun soit marié.

Passevent: Je te prometz que tout ce qu'ilz font extérieurement et en apparence, ce n'est que pour tromper et abuser le monde, et entretenir telle justice, et ceux qui l'administrent. Car si bien tous sont mariez, les bourdeaux sont par les fossés de Genève, Lausanne, et autres villes, sans les putains qui sont par les cabaretz, et maisons. Mesmement à Lausanne, la belle

> Marguerite de Lorraine, et la belle Magdelaine, femme du sonneur de cloches, et la belle lingère de la mercerie, femme du peintre, qui se tient la plus secrète, et qui par saint Françoys, ne le fait qu'un à la fois. (#69, p. 29-30)

Pasquin presses for further gossip:

> Et dy moy un peu la vie de telles paillardes, si elles sont du pais, ou si elles sont venues là, pour prendre la réformation Evangélique, et de quel lieu elles sont parties: et premièrement de la belle Marguerite de Lorraine?
>
> *Passevent:* La belle Marguerite est venue de Metz, en Lorraine, de là où elle s'est séparée de son mary, bien riche, pour s'abandonner à un Capitaine François, qui l'a tenue en garnison en sa chambre neuf mois. Et voiant que son mari la faisoit chercher vifve ou morte, luy craignant sa peau, la fist conduire par un petit laquaiz à Lausanne aux Evangéliques qui tout reçoivent (mesmement s'ilz sont riches), et là retrouva un orfèvre qui se dict son oncle: là où elle tient son bordeau, bien richement accoustrée, tant en robbes de fin drap noir, escarlate, et violet, comme en demy-ceint d'argent de valeur de vingt cinq ou trente francz, et avec dix ou douze aneaux d'or garnis de pierrerie, à ses doigts: .... et son livre de psalmes ou nouveau Testament bien dorez, dessouz son bras, se va présenter tous les jours au sermon, et prend le lieu devant le prêcheur, le plus propre pour monstrer son visage bien fardé. Et puis le reste du temps à qui en veut pour son argent. Et si quelque bon personnage en parle à Viret, le grand paillard de l'Eglise de Lausanne luy respond qu'elle a laissé son mary comme Papiste et idolâtre, pour venir à l'Evangile de Jesuchrist, qui est venu pour les pauvres pécheurs, et non pas pour les justes. Et je t'assure que si Viret n'y sentoit prouffit, bien tost la ville d'elle, et de ses compaignes en seroit nettoiée. (#69, p. 30-31)

One other case, that of Mathurin Cordier, will adequately illustrate the method of the author of this pamphlet:

> *Passevent:* Je te diray maintenant la vie d'un vieillard comme un des tesmoings de Susane, qui est le principal du Collège, et des Ecoles publiques, nommé Mathurin Cordier, qui au passé

estoit prestre en l'Eglise de Nostre Dame de Bonnes nouvelles de Rouen. Iceluy est allé à l'Evangile, avecques trois nepveux et une niepce (ou bien mieux et à la vérité, les nepveux à ses frères), et pour couvrir mieux la chose, l'un d'eux se fait nommer Brunet, et les autres deux avecques la niepce se font appeler Pelaiz.

Pasquin: Ilz sont donc ses fils et bastards: ce néantmoins se font nommer de divers surnoms pour mieux tromper ceux-là du païs, et autres.... (#69, p. 62-63)

Passevent: Je cognois que tu m'entens, que telz nepveux sont les propres enfans et bastards à Mathurin Cordier, veu que journellement il ne cesse de conquester, et acquérir maisons en Lausanne, et vignes et terres au dehors; le tout à leur nom, et cecy il fait de l'argent, qu'il desrobe sus le salaire des Régens du college.... (#69, p. 63)

The foregoing passages provide an idea of the style and content of the pamphlet, which passes in review most of the important names in the reformed church cities of Switzerland. The private lives of Théodore de Bèze, Viret, Farel and several dozen others are copiously described in scurrilous terms which bear little relation to the truth.

* * *

The *Passevent parisien* has been attributed from the time of its first publication both to Artus Désiré and to Antoine Cathelan. The authority for both attributions is worthy of consideration: Du Verdier listed it among the works of Cathelan,[1] whose name appeared (according to Brunet) on one edition published at Lyon; but in the *Comédie du pape malade*, Artus Désiré, "l'affamé," introduced himself as:

> Ce grand poete et fort savant
> Qui a fait ce beau Passavant.[2]

---

[1] Du Verdier, III, 99.
[2] Shaw, lines 1383-4.

Subsequent commentators have attributed the work now to one, now to the other, depending on which authority they consulted or were willing to accept. Liseux, in his reedition of the work in 1875, maintained a strict neutrality, while Cioranesco in his bibliography of the 16th century listed it once under the name of Cathelan, once under that of Désiré. Alfred Cartier, in an article devoted to Désiré's *Grandes chroniques et annales*, considered the question carefully, and concluded that Cathelan was the author.[3] But Miss Helen Shaw, in her critical edition of the *Comédie du pape malade*, found that the weight of evidence pointed to Désiré.[4]

There are important reasons for rejecting Désiré as the author, and for accepting Cathelan. Principal among these is the righteous indignation Désiré usually displayed at the alleged licentiousness of the leaders of the reformed church. He had accused the same individuals of the same misconduct as that represented in the *Passevent*, for example, the seduction of nuns by undignified renegades from the Catholic fold. But characteristically Désiré raged and stormed at such behavior, and grieved at the desecration of the "sanctimoniales." The attitude implicit in the *Passevent* is quite different. The author takes a malicious delight in reporting the supposed misconduct of the Genevan leaders. There is no anger in his narration, merely a cynical relish at the effrontery of the leaders, and the gullibility of the followers. This difference alone might justify rejecting Désiré as the author.

According to information supplied by Calvin[5] and Théodore de Bèze,[6] Antoine Cathelan was a young *cordelier albigeois*, who

---

[3] Cartier, p. 170.
[4] Shaw, p. 146n.
[5] Calvin, *Oeuvres françoises*, p. 314.
[6] De Bèze, *Vie de Calvin*, p. 111. "Ceste année-la, il composa le petit livret intitulé *Reformation pour imposer silence à un certain belistre, nommé Antoine Cathelan, jadis cordelier d'Albigeois*. L'occasion fut, que cet homme là avec une sienne putain estant ici venu, fut incontinent cognu tel qu'il estoit, à scavoir un affronteur, et pourtant contraint de desloger. Et puis s'estant retiré à Lausanne et aux terres de Berne, fit tant par ses beaux actes, qu'il en fut banni sur peine du fouët. Or cela le despita tellement, que s'en estant retourné en France, il fit imprimer une certaine epistre, intitulée *A Messieurs les sindiques de Genève*, en laquelle il detractoit de la doctrine de Calvin, aussi de l'Eglise et escole de Lausanne..." The report of Calvin

drifted into Geneva with his "putain," was quickly recognized for the dissolute adventurer that he was, and was driven out. He next went to Lausanne, where he enrolled in the local college, but quickly displayed such a total ignorance of the Latin he professed to know that he was again forced to leave. We further learn from Du Verdier [7] that having returned to France, he issued a challenge to Calvin to debate the question of the "sacrements de l'autel"; and from Calvin himself, that Cathelan's pamphlet contained charges closely resembling those of the *Passevent*.[8] Thus Cathelan, departing from Protestant territory with rancor against Calvin and other leaders, might have avenged himself by attributing to his enemies those very shortcomings with whose nature he was most familiar, that is, his own. Although by no means conclusive, the evidence here points toward Cathelan as the author of the *Passevent parisien*.

Another reason for doubting the attribution to Désiré is the style of the work. Désiré wrote mostly in verse, but occasionally he produced a pamphlet, or part of a pamphlet, in prose. His prose in such cases is usually ponderous and inept, with a tendency towards the apocalyptic. By contrast the style of the *Passevent* is rather light and fast moving, as befitted the malicious attitude of the narrator. The slanders of the *Passevent parisien* resemble those of Artus Désiré, but they are recounted with a malice and a deftness of style unfamiliar in the latter.

The question of authorship should probably rest here, were it not for several little facts which continue to link Désiré with the work:

1. Désiré appears to claim *Passevent parisien* for his own in the author's prologue to the *Regretz, complaictes et lamentations d'une damoiselle*, which he is known to have composed. In this prologue, Passevent again communicates with "Pasquin romain," as follows: "Mon compagnon et amy Pasquin, pource qu'il y a deux ans passez que n'as

---

is fuller than that of de Bèze; but since it is not Cathelan who is at issue here, his remarks may be omitted.

[7] Du Verdier, loc. cit.

[8] Calvin, p. 315. "Il dit que j'ai entretenu une nonnain, laquelle on m'a dit que j'ai vue une fois seulement..." for example.

receu aucunes nouvelles de moy, ne moy de toy, sachant bien aussi que seras tres joyeux de scavoir et entendre comme c'est porté par de ça de puys que je ne te vy..." Here Désiré makes a clear claim to authorship, although such a move on his part might simply indicate a desire to capitalize on the success of another author's work.

2. In the *Comédie du pape malade* (1561) Désiré is named the author, despite the fact that in 1560, in the *Cuisine papale,* the work is apparently attributed to Cathelan. [9]

3. In the *Grandes chroniques et annales* Passepartout refers to "Guillot" Passevent of the earlier work, [10] although nowhere in that work was Passevent called "Guillot." Désiré himself, however, was about to give the name to a new battler for the church, "Guillot le porcher."

4. Artus Désiré was given to the practice of sometimes weaving his name into the opening lines of his works. Thus for example in the *Deffensoire* he begins:

> J'ay desiré, et tant plus je desire,
> Plus grand desir j'ay de corrompre l'ire,
> Et la fureur d'un tas de murmurans
> Contre la Foy, jour et nuict desirans
> Vivre en erreur et d'un desir ireux,
> Tendent aux fins d'un faux coeur desireux...
> (#9, f°. Avi recto)

Similarly the *Combatz* opens with the lines:

> Quand viendra le temps desiré
> Qu'on voirra par contrition
> L'homme joueur aux deiz iré
> Reprendre en soy correction?
> (#17, f°. Aiiii recto)

---

[9] Shaw, p. 146n.
[10] "N'as tu point veu la grand chronique
Qu'en a fait un bon catholique
Qu'on nomme Guillot Passevent..."
(#73, p. 3)

In view of this tradition, one is struck by the opening sentence of the *Passevent:* "Tu sois le bien retourné du voiage, à moy et à plusieurs autres désiré."

None of these apparent connections between Artus Désiré and the *Passevent parisien* prove him to have been in fact the author. But they leave enough doubt as to his role, so that it is not safe to discount entirely his collaboration. It is for that reason that the book has been considered here.

XIV. *Grandes chroniques*

Whether or not Désiré had any part in the writing of the *Passevent parisien,* he found its subject a fruitful one for further development, for in 1558 he published his *Grandes chroniques et annales de Passepartout, Chroniqueur de Geneve,* etc., in which he further developed the accusations undertaken in the earlier work. Passepartout this time is back from Geneva and reporting to his friend Pierre du Quignet, and he begins with warm praise for the other work:

> N'as tu point veu la grand Chronique
> Qu'en a fait un bon catholique,
> Qu'on nomme Guillot Passevent,
> Qui passe par là bien souvent
> Pour voir leur maniere de vivre?
>   N'as tu point veu ce plaisant livre
> Qu'il a fait de leur pauvre vie?
> Si tu ne l'as veu, je te prie
> Achete le et le regarde:
> Car c'est un bon livre de garde,
> Qui te pourra beaucoup servir
> A redarguer et à fuyr
> Les meschans pleins d'orgueil et d'ire....
>   (#73, p. 3)

He then deplores the laxity of the persecution in France, in terms which are frequently to be found in Désiré; he is disturbed especially:

> .... De voir par tout nostre païs
> Tant d'heretiques repandus,
> Sans estre bruslez ne pendus,

Non plus qu'à Geneve et à Basle.
C'est grand pitié, chascun en parle
Chascun murmure de cela.

(#73, p. 6)

Margin notations scattered through the book outline the subject-matter treated:

1) D'un jeune cordelier d'Angiers rendu à Geneve

2) De l'origine de Calvin

3) D'un bon tour que fit la femme d'un marchant de Geneve au dit Calvin

4) D'Abel Popin predicant de Geneve

5) D'un apostat Jacobin de Nantes (named Delouba)

6) D'un meschant tour que fit une femme hereticque à son valet pour ce qu'il estoit bon chrestien

7) De la mort de mademoiselle la Budee, qui mourut à Geneve

8) D'un plaquart diffamatoire apposé contre madame saincte Geneviefve

9) De deux advocatz de Bourges retirez à Geneve (brothers Colladon)

10) D'une malheureuse femme nommée patoreau de la ville de Bourges

11) D'une Bourgeoyse de Moulin

12) D'un riche paillard de Bloys nommé des Moulins

13) De Robt Estienne

The slander of the leading personages of Geneva is as implausible as in the *Passevent parisien,* but the style, in octosyllabic verse, is not nearly so incisive, and the quality of the argument is sometimes inept. The following observation from the cordelier of Angiers for example, can only redound to the credit of the Geneva administration:

> Alors tout melencolieux
> Il me dist que les Genevoys
> L'avoyent nourry pres de deux moys:
> Mais qu'il y aloit tant de pauvres,
> Que l'argent commun de leurs cofres
> Ne pouvoient à tous satisfaire.
> (#73, p. 15)

One of the most interesting features of the work is the anecdote of the reconversion of "Mlle Budee," a story to which he was to return in various works.

According to this anecdote, related by Passevent to Pasquin in the separate edition (No. 78, Chap. II), when the "demoiselle" was:

> ... à l'article de la mort
> La saint Esprit la radressa,
> Et à sa fille s'adressa
> En luy disant à haute voix
> Fille et amye je m'en voys
> Devant le jugement de Dieu,
> Lequel me admoneste en ce lieu
> De retourner par voye humaine,
> A la sainte Eglise Rommaine...
> (#73, p. 63)

The daughter runs to fetch Calvin, whom the lady then addresses as follows:

> Or la cause et raison pourquoy
> J'ay bien voulu parler à vous,
> C'est pour confesser devant tous
> Que la loy par Luther trouvée
> Est fausse, inique et reprouvée....
> .... je puis juger seurement
> Qu'il n'y a que la paillardise
> Qui les separe de l'Eglise....
> (#73, p. 65)

Whereupon she brings up all the arguments ever used by Désiré to prove the falsity of the new religion. She further declares her desire to consult a priest:

> Et veulx mourir vraye chrestienne
> En la sainte Foy catholique....
> (#73, p. 72)

Calvin reacted to her announcement in predictable fashion:

> Or quand le paillard scismatique
> Eut entendu ces propos là,
> Il luy respondit sur cela,
> Va meschante infame maudite,
> Malheureuse femme interdite,
> Va à tous les diables d'enfer,
> Va es prisons de lucifer....
> (#73, p. 72)

And they left her to die. She then prays to all the saints to intercede in her behalf, and confesses all her sins:

> Voyla comme la povre femme
> Rendit à nostre Seigneur l'ame
> En larmoyant à grosse goutte....
> (#73, p. 78)

whereupon Pasquin rejoins

> S'il est ainsi je ne fais doubte
> Qu'elle ne soit en bon chemin
> (#73, p. 78)

So that the reader may have no doubt of the infamy of Calvin, it is stated that:

> Il fut ordonné que son corps
> Seroit porté à la voirie,
> Ce qui fut fait par grand furie
> Au veu et sceu de tout le monde....
> (#73, p. 78)

The book occupies an important place in his sequence of direct assaults on the leaders of the Geneva community. In addition to his possible role as propagator if not author of the *Passevent parisien*, he is responsible for the *Disputes de Guillot*; for the debates between Calvin and de Bèze which were added to the *Disputes de Guillot* in 1560, and thereafter formed a regular part of the volume; for the *Grandes chroniques* itself; and for the extract from that work published separately as the *Regretz,* etc.... *d'une damoiselle.*

All of these works, published between 1556 and 1560, form part of a larger pattern of attacks on the Genevans (as distinct from the new religion) during much the same period, including the casual remarks in du Bellay's Geneva sonnets, and the crude slanders of Jodelle, among others.

The importance attributed to Désiré's role in this continuing controversy is proven by the frequency of the counterattacks directed against him, both individually and in company with others. There are four principal works of which Désiré is either the principal target, or one of the targets.

1. *Response au livre d'Artus Désiré intitulé: Les Grandes Chroniques et Annales*, etc., by Jacques Bienvenu — 1558. (See above Chap. II, No. XIV.)

2. *La Comédie du pape malade* — 1561 — in which Désiré is one of several Catholic pamphleteers under attack. (See above chapter I.)

3. *Le singulier antidote contre le poison des chansons d'Artus Désiré* — 1561. (See below, this chapter, under *Contrepoison.*)

4. *Satyres chrestiennes de la cuisine papale* — 1560.

In the last-named work, attributed both to Conrad Badius and to Pierre Viret, Artus Désiré is repeatedly linked with Antoine Cathelan, Pierre Doré, and others:

> ... preux Catelan Fripelipes,
> Grand docteur, grand macheur de tripes
> Et puis ce badin Deschiré
> De ses semblables desiré ....
> De ceux la qui PASSENT PAR TOUT,
> Nommez les fols iusques au bout.
> Et toy Guillot, et tes pourceaux,
> Et toy asne adoré des veaux,
> Colin Garguille, ou bien Garnier,

> Martinet, valeur d'un denier....
> Monsieur le grand docteur Raillard,
> Autrement le bougre Maillard:
> Monsieur le singe PASSAVANT
> Asne derriere, asne devant,
> Autrement Antoine du Val,
> Grand asne faisant du Cheval....
>
> (p. 45-46)

It is interesting that the works of Désiré mentioned here are the very ones directed against Geneva: Passepartout was his spokesman in the *Grandes chroniques,* and Guillot, of course, is the hero of the *Disputes.* Cathelan is mentioned, but not associated with a specific work; on the other hand, *Passevent parisien* appears to be attributed to "Antoine du Val." But this may be another name for Antoine Cathelan, for the reference to "asne derriere, asne devant" could allude to the spelling of his name ANtoine CathelAN.

Later, a group of "docteurs de Sorbonne" gathered at table, conclude that this band of Catholic apologists have done more harm than good to their cause:

Mess. Nicaise: Voyla sans faute un mot doré!
                     Y fust frere PIERRE DORÉ

Frere Thibaud: O grande consolation!

Mess. Nicaise: O certaine approbation
                     De la saincte foy catholique!

Nostre Maistre: Vive des verres la musique.
                     Changeons de propos, quelle nouvelle?
                     Que fait de Luther la sequelle?
                     Mourront-ils pas l'un de ces iours?

Mess. Nicaise: Fidam mean ils vont tousjours,
                     Et pleust à Dieu qu'on eust fait tresves.

Nostre Maistre: O le bel escosseur de febves
                     Que frere ANTOINE CATELAN!

Frere Thibaud: Baille luy belle, que de l'an
                     Il n'eust tant songé ce badin.

Nostre Maistre: Et DEMOCHARES ce dandin,
                     Et ce bel ARTUS deschiré,

Mess. Nicaise: Par diam, i'eusse desiré
Qu'ils eussent eu fiebvre quartaine,
Plustost que de prendre la peine
D'exposer par leurs menteries
Tout nostre faict a mocqueries....
(p. 117)

To underline the character of each of the four Catholic propagandists, a margin note is devoted to each:

1. Pierre Doré — tres digne Iacopin.

2. F. Antoine Catelan condamné pour bougre en son couvent d'Alby, foitté pour adultere au couvent de l'observance à Toulouse, par importunité de ceux ausquels il touchoit, depuis devenu Maistre Aliboron en Italie, et de là ayant contrefaict l'Evangeliste avec une putain par l'espace de deux ans, par faute de trouver qui s'en voulust servir, devenu piller de la foy Catholique.

3. N. Maistre de Mouchy, maistre fol iuré, tesmoin le crucifix de Noyon.

4. Artus beau faiseur de lardoires qui remaille pour avoir sa lippie.

Goujet mentions still another Protestant pamphlet, *Thrasibule Phénice* (1561), in which Désiré was held up to ridicule. It is clear from his description of the work, however, that he refers to the *Comédie du pape malade*[1] by Badius. Although Quérard lists "Thrasibule Phénice" as a pseudonym for Théodore de Bèze,[2] who is usually considered to have had at least a part in the composition of the *Pape malade*, the name is accepted today as applying to Conrad Badius. In any case, we are not dealing here with a different work.

---

[1] Goujet, XIII, 141-3.
[2] Quérard, *Supercheries littéraires*, III (1870), col. 99.

3. Hymnes composed by Artus Désiré, and his polemics against Marot's translations of the Psalms.

VI. *Hymnes ecclésiastiques*

This collection of "Hymnes en François" is one of Désiré's more ambitious works. As its title indicates, its basic ingredient is a series of 58 hymns, not translated from the Latin originals, but adapted, and designed to be sung to traditional church airs: "...j'ay bien voulu mettre en lumiere ces Hymnes sans avoir rien translaté, mais prins seulement le chant sur celles qu'on chante ordinairement en ladite Eglise."

A selection of lines from several hymns will give an idea of Désiré's style:

"Hymne de l'advent sur le chant de *Conditor alme syderum*":

>Au tribunal de deité
>Où presidoit la trinité
>Fut consulté le grand procez
>Qu'Adam forma par son excez
>La fut predit et decreté
>De par le juge omnipotent
>Que pour l'oster de pauvreté
>Donroit un plege competent
>... ... ...
> Le filz de Dieu voyant l'arrest
>Au president a respondu
>Seigneur prenez moy: je suis prest
>D'estre pour luy en croix pendu....
>   (#46, f°. 6 recto)

Again, "Autre Hymne sus *Verbum supernum prodiens*":

>Quand Dieu tout le monde ordona
>Et qu'il crea le pere Adam
>Grans dons de grace luy donna
>Qu'aussi tost perdit à son dam.
> La femme il forma de ses os
>Pour estre tous deux alliez

> Et leur dict ces gracieux motz
> Croissez et vous multipliez....
>
> (#46, f°. 7)

There follows the whole history of the temptation and fall from grace.

A third selection, "Des confesseurs, Et premierement de Sainct Nicolas sus *Pange lingua gloriosi*":

> Jeunes enfans humbles et doux
> Domenez joye et soulas
> En chantant ceste hymne à genoux
> Du benoist saint Nicolas
> Qui est à l'exemple de nous
> Solennisé icy bas....
>
> (#46, f° 66 verso)

All the editions of this collection except the one published as *Plaisans et armonieux cantiques* in 1561, contain a second set of sacred songs: ten "Chansons spirituelles," utilizing the music and parodying the words of some popular songs of the day. The first model was entitled "Vous perdez temps de me dire mal d'elle," which Désiré recast under the title "Vous perdez temps de blasmer la pucelle"; and again at random, "Resjouissez vous bourgeoises jeunes dames de Lyon" became "Resjouissez vous pucelles filles de devotion."

All the editions likewise contain a Prologue exhortatif; but again the one labeled *Plaisans et armonieux cantiques* is unique, in that its prologue calls the work a "second contrepoison" to the "chansons" of Marot. In our discussion below of his *Contrepoison* this reference will be treated more fully.

The Troyes edition, undated, contains two little addenda not found in any other edition. The first of these, "De la necessité d'obeyr à Dieu..." proposes the abandonment of "curiosity" in favor of obedience. The second, "Comment Dieu rendra au dernier jour à chacun selon ses œuvres...," emphasizes the doctrinal point that "works" will be considered on judgment day, in opposition to the Calvinist position that God's grace was sufficient, and was not affected by good works, since the soul is already predestined at birth either for salvation or damnation.

By far the most interesting feature of this work is another long discourse,* of which large selections are identical with the prologue of the 1550 edition of the *Deffensoire,* and which contains a fairly complete catalogue of his ideas and recommendations. The following aspects of the essay deserve note:

1. The original and still continuing responsibility of women for the world's ills is again emphasized:

   "Adonc ladite femme friande et curieuse de trop savoir (comme sont aujourd'huy nos diabologiennes) en print et en fit manger à son mari Adam, de sorte qu'elle mit tout le monde à l'aventure, et furent chassez du lieu de volupté. Semblablement les serpens heretiques ennemis de Dieu deçoivent et tentent les pauvres gens de legere cervelle et principalement femmes...."

   (#47, f°. M verso)

2. He makes explicit a sexual explanation of the rebellion against the church:

   "Et pour certain tous les apostats, et semeurs de ceste zizanie, ne preschent la doctrine de Luther, sinon afin qu'il leur soit permis d'avoir femme avec eux...."

   (# f°. N5 verso)

3. The death of Luther is described in harrowing detail:

   ".... je suis asseuré par gens de bien, qui estoient en la ville où il faisoit sa residence le jour qu'il rendit son ame au diable, que le matin fist une predication toute pleine de blasphemes, et la plus abominable et detestable contre l'honneur de la glorieuse vierge sacrée Marie, qu'il est possible d'ouyr, disant, en cholere, qu'il estoit tenté jusques là, de dire qu'il n'estoit point de Dieu, et apres ceste grande fureur tout fumeux et eschauffé d'heresie: sentant les tourments qui luy estoient preparez en Enfer, se retira en sa maison sur son lict, ou fut estranglé du diable, et sa paillarde couchée aupres de luy toute transie et esperduë du bruict qu'elle ouyt."

   (#47, f°. M5 verso)

---

* This discourse appears in all editions I have seen except the *Plaisans et armonieux cantiques;* but I do not know if it is included in *Hymnes ecclés.* of. 1553.

4. Despite such clear signs of divine displeasure at the heretics, Désiré concedes that:

> "... depuis peu de temps le diable a gaigné les trois parts du peuple,"

truly an astounding proportion, if the figure is to be believed.

5. Désiré quotes the testimony of others, rather than his own observation, for the sad lot of the refugees in Geneva:

> "Et je m'en rapporte à plusieurs gens de bien qui ont esté jusques audit lieu, et qui ont veu comme ils sont traitez en grande pauvrete et misere. Et mesmement gens qui estoient constituez en grands offices et dignitez, sont pour ce jourd'huy conquis et belistres, les uns tisserans, les autres tenneurs, les autres savetiers, et Dieu sçait les regrets et lamentations qu'ils font..."
>
> (#47, f°. N4 verso)

This statement is interesting for two reasons: a) It contradicts the preface to the *Combatz*, in which he claimed as early as 1550 to have visited Geneva himself; and b) it reflects considerable credit on individuals who were willing to face economic sacrifice for their religious convictions, a sacrifice which Désiré seems to have been incapable of understanding.

6. He adds significantly to his other statements on the damage done to the Church by prelates without vocation, whose only interest in their benefices is the wealth they can extract from them, for we see them, he says:

> ... encore non contans dudit revenu, vendre les cloches et descouvrir l'Eglise couverte de plomb, pour avoir argent, et les recouvrir de tuille et bien souvent de paille... Combien avons nous veu de nostre temps destruire de bois de haute fustaye, lesquels ont esté coupez et exposez aux oeuvres du monde par les dissipateurs qui se disent les pasteurs, et si tresfiers à raison des biens et support qu'ils ont, qui leur semble à voir, que la terre ne soit digne de les porter....
>
> (#47, f°. M8 verso)

7. In an interesting side-light, he points out the special feature of the rhyme throughout his collection of hymns:

> "... c'est toute rhyme masculine, ... il n'y a aucuns carmes feminins ..."
>
> (#47, f°. P verso)

At a moment when the alternation of masculine and feminine rhymes was generally, if not yet universally, employed, Désiré was sufficiently aware of standard practice to feel that his all-masculine verses required comment.

XVII. *Contrepoison*

From the beginning of his career Artus Désiré had nourished a special dislike of Clément Marot, for his translations of some of the Psalms of David. As early as 1550 in the *Combatz du fidelle papiste,* he subjected the other to a severe criticism, which began but did not end with the translation of the Psalms. The reasons alleged for his dislike are a curious mixture:

Antipapiste: ... Et n'esse pas chose honorable,
A ceux de bas entendement
Avoir leur nouveau testament
Translaté tout de mot à mot,
Ou bien les psaulmes de Marot
Qu'en rithme discriptes il a.

Papiste: Mon serment, tu m'allegues là
un bon docteur scientifique:
Le povre furtif heretique
Qui mourut sans estre malade
A bien monstré par sa ballade
Qu'en rithmant n'estoit qu'un badin
Car en faisant son balladin
Il a si tresmal Marotté
Que les sens du texte a osté
Par un grand scandaleux crime
Dont il eust mieux valeu qu'en rithme
Il n'eust composé de sa vie.

Antipapiste: Tu dictz cela par un envie
Pour ce qu'il couchoit mieux que toy.

Papiste: Je te confesse quand à moy,
Qu'en rithme estoit le plus scavant
Estimé du peuple vivant,
Et si son sens desordonné
Il eust aussi bien adonné
A dire chose veritables
Comme il a faict actes damnables,
S'eust esté merveilles de luy.
Mais je dy qu'il n'y a celuy
Qui ne sent de sa maladie,
Qui ne confesse et qui ne die
Qu'il tenoit la loy Lutheriste
Car s'il eust esté bon papiste
Pas il n'eust esté provocqué
Soy mocquer comme c'est mocqué
Du pere sainct à pleine voix.
Semblablement les Genevoys
N'eussent pas tenu son prologue
  Ne chanter en leur synagogue
Ses vers dessus prophanes chantz.
Dont appert qu'ilz sont bien meschantz,
D'avoir par une ambition
Delaissé la translation
De sainct Hierosme catholique
Pour prendre celle d'un lubrique
Qui se dist estre en sa facture
Plus expert en saincte escripture
Que tous les docteurs de Sorbonne.
  Il est vray que sa rithme est bonne,
Mais la fumée en sent son feu
D'avoir parlé contre le veu
D'obedience et chasteté:
Pour ce qu'il n'a pas chaste esté
Il veult que chascun luy ressemble...

(#14, f°. 12 verso-13 verso)

Thus under cross examination, what had been criticism of his translation became criticism of his character. He was a fine poet, but he was considered a "Lutheriste," and he made several damnable statements. Furthermore, he was a licentious person himself. The argument is weak and somewhat elusive; his intention was to slander by innuendo.

But the popularity of Marot's translations, sung as hymns in the reformed churches continued to grow.[1] In 1560 Désiré made a frontal attack on Marot, with publication of his *Contrepoison des cinquante deux chansons de Clement Marot, faussement intitulées par luy Psalmes de David*. A *dizain* by the author explains why he found it desirable to compose his refutation:

> Quand quelque ennemy de la Foy
> Chante les chansons de Marot
> Et qu'on luy demande pourquoy
> Il les chante, il ne respont mot,
> Sinon que le malheureux sot
> Dict qu'il vault mieux en lieu publique
> Les chanter que chansons lubriques.
> Dont a ceste cause et raison
> J'ay pour tous les bons catholiques
> Composé ce Contrepoison.
>
> (#88, f°. 8 verso)

The little work was considered worthy of the specific approval of the Faculté de Théologie, in these terms:

> Ce present livre a esté veu, visité et approuvé, par vénérables docteurs de la Faculté de Théologie de l'Université de Paris; auquel n'ont trouvé chose qui puisse empêcher l'impression d'iceluy; ains l'ont trouvé tresutile et necessaire à estre mis en lumière.... Faict et signé soubz les seings manuelz des dictz docteurs, le 20 may 1560.
>
> (#92, f°. 1 verso)

In an appeal "Aux citoyens de Geneve," with which he ends the book, Désiré explains his method of composition:

> ...Ce qui m'a incité à composer ledict Contrepoison, non par que j'aye translaté le Psalmiste: car c'est matière trop haulte et impossible à l'homme, de le mettre en rithme

---

[1] Lenoir, Paulette, *La Poésie religieuse de Clément Marot*, Paris, Nizet, 1955. p. 343: "Mais Marot a visé, et a atteint plus haut. Bientôt mis en musique puis harmonisé par de très grands artistes... ses psaumes, complétés par ceux de Théodore de Bèze, connurent une fortune qui laisse loin derrière elle celle de tous les autres recueils de vers lyriques français."

Françoyse, sans y ajouster ou diminuer. A ceste occasion j'ay changé seulement le sens des chansons dudict Marot tant pour raison des censures d'icelles, que pour vostre salut et conversion....

(#88, f⁰. 78 recto)

By his own admission, then, Désiré did not undertake to translate the original psalms, too difficult a task for mortal man, but merely produced a series of parodies of Marot's translations. To settle any doubt that this was in fact his method, we reproduce below a random sample of Marot's first psalm, together with Désiré's parody of it.

I. Marot — Pseaume I: *Beatus vir qui non abiit.* Ce pseaume chante que ceulx sont bien heureux qui, rejectans les mœurs et les conseils des mauvais, s'addonnent à congnoistre et mettre à effect la loy de Dieu, et malheureux ceulx qui font au contraire.

>Qui au conseil des malings n'a esté,
Qui n'est au trac des pecheurs arresté,
Qui des mocqueurs au banc place n'a prise,
  Mais nuict et jour la loy contemple et prise
De l'Eternel, et en est desireux,
Certainement cestuy là est heureux.
  Et si sera semblable à l'abrisseau
Planté au long d'un clair courant ruisseau,
Et qui son fruict en sa saison apporte,
  Du quel aussi la fueille ne chet morte,
Si qu'un tel homme et tout ce qu'il fera
Tousjours heureux et prospere sera....[2]

II. Désiré — ARGUMENT. Ceste chanson monstre que tresheureux sont les vrays Catholicques, qui rejectent et repoussent les Heresies de Calvin et de ses complisses assis en la chaire de pestilence. Chanson I, intitulée par le dict Marot, Beatus vir qui non abiit en consilio impiorum.

>Qui au conseil de Calvin n'a esté
Et qui ne s'est à Genesve arresté

---

[2] Marot, Clément, *Œuvres complètes*, Paris, Garnier, 1919. 2 vol. II, 310.

Pour reposer au banc de pestilence,
Mais a tousjours en grande reverence
Honnoré Dieu et ses saincts glorieux
Certainement tel homme est bienheurex
  Semblable il est à un jeune Arbrisseau
Planté au long d'un clair courant ruisseau...
Donnant son fruict en sa saison requise
Car ferme il est en la foy de l'Eglise
Dont il rapporte en ladicte saison
Les dignes fruictz de jeusne et d'oraison....

(#92, f°. 9 recto)

Désiré took each of the fifty psalms of Marot and transformed them in much the same way into a kind of diatribe against Marot, Calvin, Geneva and the "luthériens." His language is as intemperate and his versifying as inadequate as in his other works. If the unsuspecting reader should sit down with the *Contrepoison,* and without the psalms of Marot, he might occasionally be struck by the effectiveness of a line here or there. But an investigation would almost always reveal that such lines had been transplanted without change from the model of Marot.

In his eagerness to contradict the sense of Marot's translations, he went at times so far as to falsify completely the clear meaning of the original, for example:

I. Marot — Les commandements de Dieu. Exode ch. 20.

Leve le cueur, ouvre l'oreille,
Peuple endurcy, pour escouter
De ton Dieu la voix nomparei-
                [lle,
Et ses commandements gouster.
  Je suis, dit-il, ton Dieu ce-
                [leste,
Qui t'ay retiré hors d'esmoy
Et de servitude moleste:
Tu n'auras autre Dieu que moy.
  Tailler ne te feras image
De quelque chose que ce soit;

II. Désiré — Autre Chanson dudict Marot, intitulée par luy, Cantique extrait du XX d'Exode.

Garde le coeur ferme l'oreille
Peuple chrestien peur d'escou-
                [ter,
De Luther la voix nompareille
Et de sa doctrine gouster.
  Je suis (dict Dieu) ton roy ce-
                [leste
Qui ay faict l'eglise et la loy,
Pour te preserver de moleste
Et des erreurs contre la foy.
  Tailler donc feras son Image
Et des benoistz sainctz qu'il
                [conçoit,

Si honneur luy fais et hommage,   Si honneur leur fais et hom-
[mage
Ton Dieu jalousie en reçoit.... ³   De grace l'accepte et reçoit....

(#92, f°. 74 recto)

Désiré seems to have been criticized for his accusation of heresy against Marot, for in a second edition of the *Contrepoison*, published in 1561, he added a new preface, entitled "Des heresies et blasphemes de Clement Marot, et des causes pour lesquelles avons intitulé ce present livre Contrepoison," and a separate article listing the "lieux et passages où Marot a erré, et maltraduict la saincte Escripture." In the first of these he defends himself vigorously against those "ennemys de la foy," his critics:

> Pour raison que par cy devant, plusieurs ennemis de nostre Religion Chrestienne, empoisonnez du mortifere venin de Clement Marot, se sont grandement scandalisez et tourmentez en leurs espritz de ce qu'avons intitulé ce present livre Contrepoison, et semblablement taxé ledict Marot d'heresie et infidelité. Et par ce qu'en la premiere impression de ce dict livre, n'avons declairé les lieux et passages de ses heresies et blasphemes, pour laquelle cause ont voulu dire et soustenir que ne sçaurions donner aucun tesmoignage ne preuve suffisante, par laquelle puissions verifier nostre dire, à cause de quoy nous ont incitez respondre à leurs reproches et calumpnies, tant à leur grand honte et confusion, qu'à la reprobation, interdiction et censure de leurs chansons Marotines, aux quelles deliberons leur monstrer mainfestement et clairement ledict lieu où il se declare vray atteiste au bien tenant la foy du Juif, niant nostre sauveur Jesus Christ, estre Dieu et homme. Par mesme moyen en plusieurs passages de ses autres oeuvres se declare Lutheriste, Manichéen, Pellagien, Vigilancien, ...

(#90, f°. 7 recto)

The sequence of his claims in the two different editions of the *Contrepoison* closely parallels that of the *Combatz*: he based his original work on the unfounded claim that Marot had falsified the psalms in his translation. When asked for particulars, he then

---

³ Marot, *op. cit.*, II, 299-300.

took refuge behind a kind of shot-gun blast at the heretical statements scattered through Marot's works.

Not surprisingly, Artus Désiré was almost immediately deluged with criticism for his parodies of the psalms of Marot, and not exclusively from the anti-Catholic party. Monluc, bishop of Valence, was highly indignant at the Sorbonne doctors, who, he claimed, had

> condamné un sien livre qu'il maintiendroit estre bon et Chrestien, fait par luy pour son Clergé de Valance, et qu'au contraire ils avoient authorisé un tresmeschant et sot livre en rime d'Artus Désiré, qui avoit falsifié le second commandement de Dieu en ces termes:
>
> > Tailler tu te feras image
> > De quelque chose que ce soit,
> > Si honneur luy fait et hommage
> > Ton Dieu grand plaisir en reçoit
>
> A quoy Maillard, doyen de la faculté, n'eut autre chose à respondre sinon que quant au livre de l'Evesque de Valence ils l'en contenteroient, et quant à l'autre, qu'il le destestoit, encores qu'il approuvast les images des Chrestiens, et qu'il ne pensoit que la faculté eust veu ce livre. [4]

Thus like Désiré himself, the Faculté de Théologie was forced to retreat when challenged directly on their approval of the book. This did not prevent the work from reappearing in a number of new editions, still with the approval of the Sorbonne.

A much more serious effort was made to discredit his volume of parodies, by an anonymous poet, in a work entitled *Singulier antidote contre le poison des chansons d'Artus Désiré, ausquelles il a damnablement et execrablement abusé d'aucuns psalmes du prophete Royal David, fait par I. D. D. C. .... M.D.LXI.*

This is a frankly polemical work, whose censure of Désiré is almost as violent as Désiré's critique of Marot; the *Exhortation au lecteur* established the double purpose of his work:

---

[4] *Hist. ecclés.*, I, 778.

Aussi un autre bon pillier de Sorbonne, nommé Artus Désiré, n'en a fait envie pour le beau chef-d'oeuvre qu'il a voulu faire au dernier Caresme, duquel je me tay, pour ce que les pierres mesmes le savent. Et pour le livre sien, nommé le Contrepoison de 52 chansons de Marot, etc. se moquant de David à pleine bouche, comme un Atheiste et chien recouru à son vomissement. Tant y a que fraudes vulpines (comme seront celles du saint Pere) sont descouvertes, au profit du Roy et du Royaume: ainsi que trouverez par mes chansons....

(f°. 3)

First then, he proposed to defend Marot's translations, and refute not only Désiré's grotesque parodies, but the entire Catholic position on the theological questions dear to Désiré. His second purpose was to censure Désiré's treasonable trip towards Spain, and at the same time emphasize the layalty of the French Huguenots to their king, Charles IX. The "beau chef d'œuvre qu'il a voulu faire au dernier Caresme" is a reference to Désiré's unsuccessful effort to enlist the aid of Philippe II of Spain.

The technique of the anonymous pamphleteer parallels that of Désiré himself; that is, he parodies the parodies of the Catholic poet. The result is scarcely more inspired than Désiré's effort. Here once again is the beginning of Psalm I, this time reconstructed as a satirical weapon against Artus Désiré and his fellow conspirators:

Argument: La conspiration des Papistes, qui envoyoient Artus Désiré en ambassade au Roy des Espagnes. Leur ruyne par leurs abus descouvers. Sur le chant, Qui au conseil des malins n'a esté.

Qui au conseil des malins a esté,
Qui s'est au trac des Caphars arresté,
Qui des docteurs au banc sa place a prise,
Pour conspirer si maudite entreprinse
Contre la France, et en est desireux,
Certainement cestury est malheureux....

(f°. 7 recto)

In all, the author of the antidote parodied twenty of the poems of Désiré, and like their models these twenty dealt about equally with personalities and with questions of dogma. One other example will suffice to highlight the work of Marot, and the aims and methods of both his detractor and his defender.

I. Marot: No. XLII.

Pseaume CXIV — In exitu Israel de Aegypto

De la delivrance d'Israel hors d'Egypte, et succinctement des principaulx miracles que Dieu feit pour cela.

>Quant Israel hors d'Egypte sortit,
>Et la maison de Jacob se partit
>   D'entre le peuple estrange,
>Juda fut faict la grand' gloire de Dieu
>Et Dieu se feit prince du peuple Hebrieu,
>   Prince de grand' louange.... [5]

II. Désiré: No. 41

>Quand Jehan Calvin hors de France sortit
>Et que du Dieu de Jacob se partit
>   Pour vivre en terre estrange,
>Lors il se first grand ennemy de Dieu
>Et à Genesve alla prendre son lieu
>   Qui luy fut piteux change....

III. Anon.: f. 20Vo.

Sur le chant, Quand Israel hors d'Egypte sortit.

Argument — D'Artus Désiré envoyé par les Sorbonistes en Ambassade au Roy Philippe, descouvert à Orléans: de la proposition et disposition divine.

>Quand Desiré hors de Paris sortit
>Et pour aller en Espagne partit,
>   En ambassade estrange:
>Pres d'Orléans, sur la Loire, au milieu,
>Fut descouvert, par le vouloir de Dieu,
>   Auquel rendons louange....

Composed with the narrow purpose of ridiculing Désiré's *Contrepoison* and deploring his political plot, the *Antidote* today is as devoid of interest as its model, from which it derives its only *raison d'être*. Like most satires written in anger, this one was not of a

---

[5] Marot, *op. cit.*, II, 390.

sort, even when composed in 1561, to change many minds. But neither was the *Contrepoison* of Désiré likely to make many converts.

The year 1561 saw still another attempt on the part of Artus Désiré to discredit the psalms of Marot. Dusting off a little work he had published for the first time in 1553 as *Hymnes ecclesiastiques, traduits en ryme françoise sur les mesmes chants* and already reissued once in 1561 as *Hymnes en françois sur le chant de ceux de l'Eglise,* he stripped it of much of its accompanying polemical prose and reissued it under a third title, *Plaisans et armonieux cantiques de devotion, ... qui est un second Contrepoison aux cinquante deux Chansons de Clement Marot... Veu, visité et approuvé par venerables docteurs de la Faculté de Théologie.* In a "Prologue exhortatif au fidele Chrestien," slightly altered from its earlier form, he again claimed to have written these cantiques to counteract the "chansons" of Marot:

> .... Car ce que nous en avons faict a esté à l'intention que tous bons chrestiens n'ayant occasion de s'amuser à chanter plusieurs prophanes et reprouvées chansons, et entre les autres celles de Clement Marot, ausquelles ses presens cantiques serviront de second Contrepoison....
> (#48, f°. 3 verso)

Since, except for these two scant references to Marot, the work reproduces integrally the earlier editions of the *Hymnes,* it must be considered as a hasty attempt to keep his anti-Marot campaign alive, or perhaps an effort to sell his earlier book by relating it to a current controversy.

Finally in the *Singerie des Huguenots,* of 1574, he issued a final blast at Marot:

> Baise * (i.e. Th. de Bèze) a veu semblablement qu'en nostre dicte Eglise y avoit un Chant ecclesiastique, d'hymnes, proses, respons, cantiques, legendes et psalmodies, lesquelles il a contrefaictes et renversées, par un tas de folles chansons scandaleuses et prophanes, composées d'un Clement Marot, qui a grandement travaillé à la controversion d'icelles pour donner plaisir de damnation ausdicts Singes, qui ne sçavoient que dire ne chanter en leur Synagogue Lutherienne auparavant qu'il les eust mises en

lumiere: mais depuis qui les ont euës en usage, ils se sont efforcez de les publier et chanter à voix tubale et gorge desployée, pour faire oublier et cesser l'armonie des susdicts chans ecclesiastiques, tant bien ordonnez et à propos selon les temps, qu'ils excitent souvent le peuple à larmes, pleurs et devotion oyant les orgues respondre au service divin, au lieu desquelles ils usent de violons, lucs, guiternes, et autres instruments provocquans à ladicte luxure et paillardise, pour resjouïr lesdictes guenons montéés sur les crouppes de leurs grans chevaux, en allant aux presches, synodes, et prieres faitces hors la foy de l'Eglise....

(#108, f°. 8 verso)

Obviously he has not changed his views in any way since the *Combatz;* and his arguments are just as unfair in this case as they were at that time.

4. Miscellaneous Pamphlets

IX. *Description philosophale*

This insignificant work is chiefly interesting in that it shows how Artus Désiré used everything that came to hand for his own singleminded purpose.

A typical layout follows: *Du Renard.*

1) Huitain, by the original poet:

> Le Renard fin et cauteleux,
> Faict aux poulles forte bataille.
> En temps obscur et nebuleux,
> Il destruict beaucoup de volaille;
> Et en quelque quartier qu'il aille,
> Aussi tost qu'il est arrivé
> Il se jette sur la poulaille,
> Contrefaisant le chien privé.
> (#61, p. 54)

2) Picture of an evil-looking fox;

3) *Huitain*, by Artus Désiré: *Moral*

> Le dict Renard est un fin hoste,
> Plein de cautelle et piperie,
> Qui le bien des pauvres gens oste
> Par sa finesse et tromperie,
> A bien parler c'est un droit monstre,
> Qui tousjours derober est prest,
> Et par son astuce se monstre
> Estre plus fidelle qu'il n'est.
> (#61, p. 54)

4) The facing page, is devoted to a description in prose of the fox.

In his moral on the fox, Désiré resorted to the material of the *Loyauté conscientieuse des taverniers*. The vipère represents for him the heretics, in an image he was to use again in the prologue to the *Hymnes en françois*.

1) *Huitain* by the original poet:

> Une vipere proprement,
> Conçoit par la gueule son fruict,
> Puis serre les dents fermement,
> Dont le masle estrangle et destruict,
> Pour sortir les petits luy mangent
> Le ventre, dont leur pere vengent:
> Et pource on dit que la Vipere
> Ne vit jamais pere ne mere.
>
> (#61, p. 56)

2) Picture of a viper.

3) *Huitain* par Désiré: *Moral*

> Par la vipere veneneuse,
> Qui faict mourir sa mere propre,
> S'entend la secte malheureuse
> De Luther plein de grand opprobre:
> Par une grosse tyrannise
> Ses faux supposts veulent manger
> Le ventre de leur mere Eglise
> A leur grand peril et danger.
>
> (#61, p. 56)

In a like manner, after a *huitain* on the destructive feeding habits of the goat, Désiré added his *Moral*, which likened the goat to "Les femmes impudiques luxurieuses,"

> Qui au grand peril de leurs ames
> Sont des jeunes gens amoureuses:
> Les jeunes plantes elles broustent,
> C'est à scavoir jeunes enfans,
> Et tant de leur substance goustent,
> Qu'ils en meurent devant leurs ans.
>
> (#61, p. 68)

In all there are forty-eight animals, and the same number of birds, each with its little eight-line moral.

XII. *Regretz.... trespas ... Françoys Picart.*

In this work Désiré adopted an elevated style quite unlike anything he attempted before or since. The explanation is not hard to find. On September 17, 1556, occurred the death of François Picard, docteur de Sorbonne, with whom Désiré was probably acquainted, and whom he certainly admired. Sometime soon after his death there appeared the little work attributed by Barbier to d'Aubusson, listed in Chapter II above as Deploration, etc., eulogizing Picard. Whether this suggested to Artus Désiré a genre he had not attempted; whether he sincerely regretted not having first thought of eulogizing Picard; whether he merely saw a new opportunity to air his views; whatever the reason may have been, Désiré published one year later, on the first anniversary of the man's death, his own eulogy, based squarely on the work of his predecessor, but much more colorful and imaginative in its presentation of the events.

According to Désiré's model, Picard had died an ordinary death; but Désiré described the event with considerable drama: Picard preached twice that very day on the virgin Mary; this gave him a chance to contrast his death with that of Luther, strangled by the devil after preaching *against* Mary. (See *Hymnes...*, VI)

D'Aubusson described in moderate terms the mourning of the family. Désiré was more emphatic in expressing sympathy for Picard's sister:

> Plorez, gemissez tendrement,
> Et d'un coeur triste et vehement
> Aydez par une grand' douceur,
> A plorer à sa povre soeur....
>
> (#71, f° Bii recto)

He then used the alleged virtue of this woman as an excuse for a diatribe against women's fashions:

> Delaissez vos mirelifiques
> Vos superflus habillemens,
> Vos beaux atours et ornemens...
> Jectez au diable tous vos coffres
> Pleins d'ordure et de vanitez...
> Jectez au feu ces vertugalles,

> Ces senteurs de musc et de roses
> Et au lieu de toutes ces choses
> Sentez l'ordure et fetulence,
> Qui sort de vostre conscience
> Pleine de vitupere et honte...
>
> (#71, f°. Bii verso)

Finally d'Aubusson described a decent funeral escort of clergy, family and some citizens. According to Désiré, the whole city turned out in the greatest display of mourning ever seen:

> As tu point veu toutes les rues
> Pleines de peuples haut et bas
> Criant, plorant, disant helas
> Paris, combien as tu perdu?
>
> (#71, f°. Aii verso)

In addition to the similarities of organization, there are striking examples of the same rhetorical devices:

1) Both authors indulged heavily in such words as "plorez" and "gemissez."

2) D'Aubusson interrupted a "deploration" to insert:

> Que dy je helas? estre melancholique
> Il ne convient....

In like manner Désiré interrupted himself to inquire rhetorically:

> Comment plorer, et que dis-tus
> Un homme de si grand' vertu
> Et si humain que cestuy la,
> Et nous fault il plorer ce la?
> Non....
>
> (#71, f°. Ciii recto)

And they agree that weeping is out of place because of the eternal felicity he has surely gained...

The most plausible explanation for this departure from his usual style is the assumption that he was imitating the model by d'Aubusson.

5. SOCIAL COMMENTARIES

IV. *Loyauté .... des taverniers*

The *Loyauté des taverniers* is one of the most curious of Artus Désiré's works. Not only does it deal with a subject outside his usual theological range; it does so in a down-to-earth, manner, which is often amusing and enlightening for the realism of its details. It is anything but a polished literary effort; what virtue it has lies in its presentation of the disreputable milieu of tavern society, with this added point of interest that it links Désiré very closely with this milieu — he speaks with the authority of an expert.

At the outset we are treated to a series of facetious dedications, the first of which in two strophes announces clearly his intention:

> Tresamplement des hostes indiscrets
> Veux discourir leurs grans abus secrets
> (#40, p. 1)

with an important reservation

> Je n'entens point parler des gens de bien,
> Qui donnent vin pour une Patenostre: ....
> (#40, p. 1)

However distant the subject may seem to be from his usual topics, there is a connection: the good innkeepers are those who contribute wine in return for a prayer.

A second dedication begins with an effort at rabelaisian humor: "A nos bien aymés et loyaux sommeliers et boutilliers, du trespuissant, et tresvertueux Roy Bacchus; L'autheur de ce présent livre Mille saluts de fin d'or d'Arabie, Pour maintenir solatieuse vie." (#40, p. 3) But his tone quicky becomes more serious, and he ends his dedication with another declaration of his intentions:

> Sommairement sans grans propos ne chants
> Declarer veux tous les abus meschans
> Des hosteliers, et trompeurs taverniers
>
> (#40, p. 5)

To judge from Désiré's words, the tavern keepers are not an edifying group:

> L'estat, et train de tous ces gens ici
> C'est d'estre assis, et manger gras morceaux
> Sans de travail avoir aucun soucy
> Et vivre ainsi comme font les pourceaux:
> Et ammasser or, argent, à monceaux,
> A droit ou tort, sans regarder comment:
> Mais d'un et d'autre empoigner fermement
> Pour un solz trois, contre Dieu et raison,
> Voyla le train et le gouvernement
> Des taverniers, tenans grosse maison
>
> > Les gourmans gloutons
> > Couvers de boutons,
> > Pour eux faire gras
> > Mordent comme rats....
>
> (#40, pp. 6-7)

Their wives and daughters do not fare much better:

> Semblablement ma dame l'hosteliere
> Pour attirer jeunes bragards de ville,
> Se maintiendra belle frisque et gorriere,
> Et par ce point remplira sa coquille
> Si elle est vieille, elle aura quelque fille
> Qu'elle mariera à quelque jeune beau,
> Et devant luy leschera le morveau
> des compaignons, qui viendront leans boire,
> Apres bon vin, se joüent au bordeau,
> Ce temps pendant jenin cuyra la poire.
>
> > Apres gourmandise
> > S'ensuit paillardise
> > Et pour le succide
> > Souvent homocide.
>
> (#40, p. 10)

Désiré's Christian objections to these dens of iniquity are spelled out in detail:

1) Tous leurs logis sont comble de blaspheme....
   (#40, p. 25)

2) Car pour certain la taverne et le jeu,
   Et le bordeau, où se commet grand mal,
   Sont proprement les ennemis de Dieu,
   Et les chemins d'aller à l'hospital....
   (#40, p. 25)

3) L'un pour enseigne aura la Trinité
   L'autre saint Jean, et l'autre saint Savin
   L'autre saint Mor, l'autre l'humanité
   De Jesus Christ nostre sauveur divin
   De Dieu des saints sont leurs crieurs de vins....
   (#40, p. 25)

4) .... pendant qu'on fait ledit service
   Sont à vacquer aux oeuvres du grand diable...
   Aux temps present on a beau leur deffendre
   De bailler vin, durant ladite messe....
   (#40, p. 29)

There is at least a hint that Désiré was annoyed at the treatment accorded to him personally. In addition to his complaint that many innkeepers no longer offered a meal for a "patenostre," he seems piqued at discourtesy of the profession, perhaps recalling an earlier period of greater respect to the clergy:

> Si en passant vous ostez le bonnet,
> En leur faisant honneur et reverence,
> Un fier regard vous donront de cornet,
> Et mesprisant vostre honneste presence:
> Et outre plus d'une folle loquence
> Se gaudiront et mocqueront de vous,
> Et fussiez vous tout vestu de veloux....
> (#40, p. 33)

But along with his outrage at the violation of Christian principles and common decency, Artus Désiré formulated an acid indictment of the tricks used to cheat the customers; this is perhaps the most interesting aspect of the work.

> Devant mes yeux j'ay veu en pleine ruë
> A une hostesse acheter sur le banc,
> Pour six deniers d'une vieille morue

> Qui ne valoit à peine pas un blanc,
> Or devinez (sans le vin ne pain blanc)
> Combien el'fut aux compaignons venduë
> Je sois maudit si la fauses pendue
> N'en feit payer deux sols et six deniers...
> Pour la cuisson de deux chapons rostis,
> De deux gigots, et bœuf boüilly aux choux
> Les rançonneurs de raison divestis
> Firent payer (comme on m'a dit) vingts sols...
>   (#40, pp. 43-44)

Many pages follow devoted to underhanded tricks used by tavern keepers to cheat their clientèle; three fourths of their price is profit; unless you bargain with them beforehand, they will overcharge; they let meat rot rather than sell it near cost; they resell leavings to the next comer; they steal from the hungry, and are therefore worse than brigands; they resell unconsumed wine; they sell gladly to anyone who has the price; they mix their wine with anything at hand to stretch it; they slip bad wine in along with the good: you pay for both:

> Esbahy suis comme l'homme a le cœur
> Boire cela qui ne vaut deux deniers...
> Il faut tousjours à la main la lanterne
> Pour triboüiller les mauvais vins qu'on forge
> A y songer, cela me rend si terne
> Qu'a bien petit que je n'en rens ma gorge....
>   (#40, p. 50)

They charge different prices depending on the alertness of their clients; they sell old wine for new; if you tip the waiter, you will get a glass of good wine, but the next glass will be bad, and he will swear your taste deceives you; tavern keepers are proud and vain, but their breath stinks. And an echo from Marot:

> Au demourant les meilleurs fils du monde....
>   (#40, p. 53)

They have other tricks; they malform pots and pans and plates so that they won't hold as much; they are more powerful than princes, because they can fleece you and you won't dare say a word; if you don't meet their price they will insult you in the street; if a man with nothing goes into the business he will soon be rich; in winter they cheat on the amount of firewood.... We have been treated to an exhaustive and probably authentic listing of the tricks of the trade.

By contrast, his proposed solution for the situation he has outlined is both flat and unrealistic; limit the clientele of the inns to *bona fide* travelers:

> Si l'on avoit une fois deffendu
> Aux taverniers d'asseoir ceux de la ville,
> Le vin seroit à bas pris descendu:
> Et au commun profitable, et utile,
> Et qui plus est, si l'on gardoit ce style,
> Vers Dieu seroit une œuvre meritoire:...
> (#40, p. 62)

On page 83 Artus Désiré, never one for brevity or concision, begins to bring his book to a close. Following several rondeaux "contre Taverniers qui brouillent les vins," there are five pages of octosyllabic couplets on the subject "Comment Satan et le Dieu Bacchus accuse les Taverniers qui brouillent le vin," then another rabelaisian touch entitled "S'ensuit la lettre d'escorniflerie, fort recreative à toutes gens, et joyeuse pour rire," and a final "Instruction de ceux qui tiennent taverne, ou hostellerie."

V. *Grands jours*

The *Grands jours du Parlement de Dieu* is an impassioned recapitulation of the ills besetting France. Much of the argument is couched in social terms, but the "religious question" is never far from Désiré's mind. He begins with characteristic directness:

> Consideré les grans maux qui se font
> Contre l'honneur du sauveur venerable
> Esbahy suis que la terre ne font
> Dessoubz les piedz du peuple miserable...
> ... ...
> Depuis vingt ans le peuple est empiré
> De la moytié (voire des quattre pars)
> Pource Dieu est contre nous tant yré
> Qu'il nous delaisse entre gros loups espars

> Les grans lyons: et pervers leopars
> Desquelz j'entens apostatz hereticques
> ... ...
> (#41, Aiii)

> Parquoy je dy veu tant de maux iniques,
> Que l'Antechrist est bien pres de noz portes.
> (#41, Aiii verso)

Only the Parlement of Paris, he adds, has saved us until now from abolition of the mass, a revealing admission of the popularity of the new religion in 1551:

> Si ce n'estoit la court parisienne
> De parlement (souveraine justice)
> En peu de temps la gent pharisienne
> Aboliroit le divin sacrifice....
> (#41, Aiii verso)

In fact, he asserted, the signs are now clear that the day of judgment is at hand. How shall we know, the disciples asked Jesus Christ, when the day is coming?

> Gardez (dist il) que ne soyez seduis,
> Car plusieurs gens de damnable renom
> En ce temps là, seront si mal conduis
> Qu'ilz corrompront tous mon divin cannon,
> Furtivement il viendront en mon nom....
> (#41, Aiv recto)

And he proceeds to list his grievances against the heretics, this time including a new argument, strangely modern:

> Ils donneront liberté si tresgrande
> Qu'ilz defendront l'ordre de mariage
> Que Jesus Christ à observer commande
> Et publieront de leurs langue friande
> Que femmes sont à tous hommes communes....
> (#41, Aviii recto)

This provides him an opportunity to detail the sins of which women are guilty, all of them stemming from curiosity, vanity, love of novelty.

His next point is that near the day of judgment people will rise in armed struggle againt each other; and he mentions recent uprisings against the king among Bordelais and Limousins. Furthermore all France for twenty years has suffered famine, pestilence and war.

The heretics, he says, base their criticism of the Church upon misconduct of the clergy. As usual Artus Désiré admits that such criticisms are founded on fact:

> Dieu tout puissant sache quant ce sera
> Qu'on les voirra reglez et enfermez
> Le peuple errant jamais ne cessera
> De murmurer tant qu'ilz soient reformez
> Car comme ay dict ilz sont si difformez
> Qu'en leur estat n'a rithme ne raison
> Et de la sont l'eresie et poison
> Qui court ce jour en Germanie et France....
>
> (#41, f°. B5 recto)

Charity is dead. The rich lead lives of "luxe" and "luxure," as do priors and monks. There is no satisfying the avarice of kings and princes. Lawsuits for money clutter the courts. The poor, in fact, are more charitable that the rich, for the latter:

> .... si froidz sont aux aumosnes qu'lz baillent
> Qu'ilz n'osent pas bien nourrir leurs enfans,
> Tant ont de peur que les biens ne leur faillent.
>
> (#41, f°. Ci verso)
>
> ... ...
> Je dy cela que depuys cinq cens ans
> Homme ne vit si grosse pauvreté:
> Car l'indigent est si for mal traicté
> Du crediteur qui l'oppresse et travaille.
>
> (#41, f°. Di verso)

A few remarks on blasphemy show the importance Artus Désiré never failed to attribute to that cardinal sin:

> La grant vertu de noblesse qui blece
> Est en blaspheme et juremens changée
>
> (#41, f°. Ciii recto)

At this point several anecdotes reinforce his sermon:

1) Two sailors were on the Loire: one swore so terribly that the other rushed up to ask, "Chair dieu, mort dieu, et pourquoy jures tu?"

(#41, f°. C4 recto)

2) Saint Louis, hearing a man swear, "luy fist percer la langue d'un fer chault."

> D'où vient cela qu'iceux hommes errans
> Ne sont punis de leurs susdictz blasphemes:
> J'ay dict que c'est pour ce que les plus grans
> Jusques au cueur en sont tachez eux mesmes...
>
> (#41, f°. C6 recto)

On balance, however, Désiré is not displeased with the situation in Paris, which houses both the Sorbonne and the Parlement:

> O qu'heureuse est la ville de Paris
> D'avoir en elle un si riche tresor
> J'entends plusieurs Catholiques espris
> De grand scavoir, trop plus precieux qu'or.
> Et qui plus est le Parlement encor
> Du Roy Chrestien, qui a toute heure est prest
> De condamner par sentence et arrest
> Les gens errans reprouvez en Sorbonne.
>
> (#41, f°. E8 verso)

VII. *Instruction Chrestienne*

This is a curious little work, written for the purpose of stamping out blasphemy. Just as his book censuring the tavern keepers was a mine of information on the tricks of that trade, so here his diatribe against swearing is a veritable lexicon of oaths:

> L'un dict à l'autre en grand audace
> Par la teste Dieu compaignon
> Voicy du vin de bonne grace
> Qui est fort excellent et bon
> L'autre respond, mort Dieu c'est mon,
> Je reny Dieu il n'est point cher,
> L'autre dict par le sang Dieu non,
> Mais chair Dieu ayons a mascher
>
> (#51, p. 5)

An even more resounding example of the oaths reported by Désiré is this one:

> Je me donne à tous les grans diables
> Corps, ame, tripes et boyaux....
> (#51, p. 5)

Since even little children are guilty of swearing, his advice was to:

> Les fesser bien pour leur descharge
> La peau du cul revient tousjours....
> (#51, p. 7)

After singling out various groups as particularly guilty, "paillardes" and "macquereaux" among them, he comes to the nobility, who by their inveterate blasphemy prove themselves to be really common. His only constructive thought in this direction was that the king might deprive such sinners of their titles.

In a dazzling display of erudition, Désiré then listed countless examples of blasphemers and their horrid fate from both old and new testaments. For the second time here he related with approval the anecdote of Louis IX punishing a blasphemer by having his tongue pierced with a red-hot rod.

* * *

On page 56 begins a little sermon on "ingratitude des mauvais riches" wholly unrelated to the foregoing "instruction:"

> Si tu veulx que ton ame herite
> Des sielz, pour les biens que tu offres
> Il te fault sans estre hypocrite
> Secretement donner aux povres....
> (#51, p. 56)

* * *

On page 58 another new subject is introduced, the poor upbringing of children. This subject, apparently unrelated to the religious controversy, was in fact an important facet of Désiré's personal philosophy. His reasoning went somewhat as follows: Parents spoil their children, with the result that children grow up, 1) vain and dissolute, 2) despising their parents, and 3) disobedient; a generation ago there was no dissent from Catholic orthodoxy, where today it is widespread: conclusion, today's children, through disobedience to their parents, have cast off the religious traditions and teachings of their parents; and are vain and dissolute; and just look at the mess the church is in. Having come to the point closest to his heart (and all discussion leads him inevitably to the ills besetting the Church), he takes the opportunity to dwell on questions far removed from raising children, to which he did not return in this work. The Church in France, he says again, as he has frequently before, suffers from a lack of proper leadership:

> Nous voyons au troppau de Dieu
> Ours, Lyons et Loups rigoreux
> Et tous les pasteurs loing du lieu
> Qui ne se soucient que d'eulx.
> Nous voyons les gens vertueux
> Qui n'ont benefice ne office,
> Et les gros asnes six pour deux
> En ont, sans faire aucun service
>
> Las, helas, n'esse pas grand honte
> Pourvoir ceulx qui ne scavent rien?
> Et ne tenir autrement compte
> De tant de docteurs gens de bien?
> Qui ont exposé tout leur bien
> Et leurs jeunes ans à l'estude?
> ... ...
> Selon justice et equité
> Les eveschiez leur appartiennent...
>
> (#51, pp. 69-70)

Although it is clear from the fanaticism of his entire career that Désiré did not write entirely or even primarily for gain, it is hard to believe that he did not have himself in mind as one of the "gens vertueux" who deserved a benefice. There is a certain irony here, for despite his limitations, he was objecting to one of the fundamental abuses within the Church in France. Two of the most ardent defenders of orthodoxy, the Cardinal de

Lorraine and Ronsard, were particularly guilty of this abuse, which provided so much ammunition for the heretics. If Désiré pleaded from a self-interested standpoint for a more equitable allocation of Church benefices, how much weaker is the position of the cardinal and the poet, who in preaching orthodoxy, pleaded at the same time for the perpetuation of their own privileges. It may be significant that Artus Désiré dedicated none of his works to the Cardinal de Lorraine, who was nevertheless in a better position to help him than perhaps any other prelate.

XXI. *Origine et source*

This pamphlet, published in 1571, the first new work published by Artus Désiré in about a decade, is composed in a new style: doggerel verse has been abandoned for apocalyptic prose. The first section echoes some ideas treated in the *Instruction chrestienne*, in which he dealt with the rearing of children, among other things. Again he makes the point that the revolution that occurred in religious affiliation from one generation to the next is attributable to the disobedience of the younger generation, which in turn stems from lack of stern discipline in their upringing: "tesmoings plusieurs miserables et malheureux peres, qui ont donné si grande liberté de conscience à leurs enfants de perdition, qu'ils sont venus à descongnoistre Dieu et à desnier toute puissance duë à leurs pasteurs et princes de la terre..."

(#102, f°. 5 recto)

The second section, which is in effect a continuation of the first, deplores the familiarity allowed between children and servants, considered to be another aspect of poor upbringing which also leads to corruption of the children.

In the third and final section, Désiré thunders at his public as from a pulpit, announcing the imminence of divine vengeance upon the French people for their persistence in sin; in so doing he returned to a subject he had first treated twenty years before in the *Grans jours du parlement de Dieu*. It is here especially that his eloquence reached impressive heights. First he details the clear signs of God's displeasure: "Or est il ainsi que depuis mille ans, le peuple ne fut visité de telle sorte qu'il a esté depuis la mort du feu Roy Henry (que Dieu absolve) jusques à ce jourd'huy...." (#102, f°. 32 recto) These signs are:

1) death of Henry II.

2) death of François II, and accession of Charles IX, "car une des grandes punitions qu'il puisse envoyer à un peuple c'est luy donner une jeune enfant pour Roy..."

(#102, f°. 32 recto)

3) the deep frost and resulting famine of the winter of 1565: "tous les elements crient vengeance contre les erreurs, sacrileges, symonies, injustice, orgueil, usure, rapine et toute sorte de vice, que nous souffrons et permettons regner sans aucune correction, et principalement infidelité et mespris de la loy de Dieu et de son Eglise, qui a esté cause de ladicte passée...."

(#102, f°. 32 verso)

He then proceeded to list in an eloquent series his grievances against various classes of his compatriots:

> O vrays fideles et Catholiques où est ce jourd'huy la saincte vie et conversation des bons Prelats et pasteurs de l'Eglise universelle? Où est l'honneur, crainte et obedience, que les Roys et Princes de la terre souloient avoir à eux, comme un Theodose à monsieur S. Ambroise? Où est l'humilité, prudence et vertu de tous les nobles, genereux et fideles gentils hommes du Royaume de France? Où est la loyauté et liberalité des bons marchands et bourgeois du passé? Où est la simplicité et patience des artisans et laboureurs rustiques? Où est la discipline reguliere des peres et meres envers leurs enfans, et l'obedience d'iceux? Où est la chaste contenance, modestie et honnesteté des vertueuses dames et damoiselles du temps passé? Où est la douceur, grace, faconde et contentement du simple estat des bourgeoises, filles et femmes de France? Où est la reformation des gens de bien en claustralle closture, et la vie et doctrine des regens et pedagogues envers leurs disciples et escoliers? Où est le temps que nostre Royaume florissoit et prosperoit en prelature et judicature, sans aucun schisme, erreur ne contradiction? Où est le temps que tout le monde s'accordoit l'un avec l'autre, beuvant et mangeant d'un mesme pain d'escrip-

ture, et d'une chair et sang de Jesus Christ au sainct sacrement de l'autel? Bref le tout est changé et tombé en confusion et damnation...

(#102, f°. 37 verso)

For special mention, he singled out "messieurs les gros Millours, Marchands et Bourgeois, qui vous elevez et glorifiez à la grandeur de vos biens... Car nous voyons en vous un si grand orgueil et mespris de vos prochains, pour l'abondance de voz mondaines richesses, qu'il vous semble advis que la terre n'est digne vous porter, tant estimez et tenez de vos personnes, par ladite maladie du diable... laquelle est si grande et enracinée... que si passe devant vous quelque pauvre Moyne croté, ou autre simple prestre qui vous saluë... par un mespris et contemnement de l'estat ecclesiastique, comme vilains ingrats superbes et ambitieux, vous leur donnez un grand coup de hochet de vostre teste escervelée, comme s'ils estoient vos subjects et inferieurs..."

(#102, f°. 39 recto)

Another diatribe is directed against young preachers, who attract larger audiences than their betters:

"Ce que nous avons veu et voyons ordinairement devant noz yeux, de plusieurs venerables docteurs sçavans et consommés en toutes sciences divine et humaines, avoir peu de personnes en leurs predications, et sont delaissez dudict peuple, pour aller ouyr et escouter un tas de jeunes plaisans veaux, qui ont la langue à commandement et nul fondement de l'escripture saincte, lesquelz sont exaltez et elevez jusques au tiers ciel, et combien qu'il n'ayent nulle edification ne grande experience ès lettres sainctes, si est-ce toutefois qu'ils ont et occupent les premiers lieux et places, et sont trop mieux venus et receuz des Auditeurs, que le plus docte et expert Theologien de ce monde pour le beau maintien, contenance, grace et faconde qui est en eux, par une vraye humilité et obedience qui vault trop mieux que sacrifice, afin aussi d'eviter ladite curiosité, qui ce jourd'huy est cause de tous nos maulx, ainsi qu'il appert par une infinité de pauvre peuple, qui s'est voulu mesler d'interpreter les sainctes escriptures et de prescher l'evangile sans jamais avoir estudié un seul mot de latin ne françois..."

(#102, f°. 42 recto-43 verso)

If only, he complains, we had prelates and judges willing to be severe in the execution of their responsabilities, our troubles would be at an end:

> "Et pource Messieurs les gens d'Eglise, Prestres, Ministres de l'autel plorez, hurlez et vous couchez dessus le sac de cendre, soyez ceins et troussez sus vos reins de la ceinture de chasteté, en regretant l'offerte et oblation du precieux corps de Jesus Christ au saint sacrement de l'autel. Voici... la famine, playe mortelle, tribulation et angoisse que Dieu vous envoye pour vous amender, et pour toutes ces afflictions, n'y a nul qui se corrige de ses offenses et pechez..."
>
> (#102, f°. 47 recto-48 recto)

The tone of this work and of those which follow has changed somewhat. His message is integrally the same, but he no longer makes orderly demonstrations of the truth of the Catholic religion. His manner is now prophetic, and the organization of his ideas has deteriorated somewhat.

XXII. *Desordre et scandale*

The substance of this book, as the title suggests, closely parallels that of his other "social" protests. The errors in religion had led to a host of other abuses, which had in turn led to errors in religion. Under attack here, as usual, are:

1) "escumeurs et corsaires" of church property;
2) "apostats" (Huguenots);
3) "laics" (holders of church benefices without vocation);
4) "blasphemateurs";
5) the wealthy, who squander money on fine clothes and do nothing to help the poor;
6) women, and their vanity and finery, "les paillardes du monde et impudiques femmes..."

(#105, f°. 33 recto)

7) "enfants presomptueux";
8) kings and princes, "Qui ont l'authorité et pouvoir d'y mettre ordre, Et toutefois sont ceux qui corrompent les droits";

(#105, f.° 39 recto)

9) "messieurs les gens d'eglise, Evesques et prelats..." who have abandoned their flocks;

10) vain preachers, more concerned with their reception by the public than with their message;

11) judges, "qui auront forvoyé contre Dieu et raison en quelque judgmens, Et par faveur ou don du bon droit devoyé..."

(#105, f°. 32 verso)

All these unrepentant sinners are threatened with the torments of hell, which are described in some twenty pages of hyperbolic verse. This passage alone would be enough to discourage the most sympathetic reader; but the clarity of the work is further obscured by a corresponding but fortunately briefer description of paradise. He dwells at length on Jonas as symbol for all those who are ruining the church from within:

> Et tout par les Ionas, qui sont (comme dict est)
> Entrez dedans la nef maugré qu'en ait eu Dieu...
> (#105, f°. 8 recto)

which sometimes adds to the confusion.

Désiré's naive effort to portray heaven and hell for his readers makes this work even less readable than his other social commentaries. Aside from these digressions, there is little that is unexpected in the book, at this advanced point in his literary career. There is, however, a strange perversion of christian charity attributed by Désiré to the blessed souls who reach heaven:

> Grande liesse ilz ont comme predestinez,
> De la damnation de leurs peres et meres,
> Et les peres aussi de leurs enfans damnez
> Sans estre contristez de leurs douleurs ameres.
>   Car la volonté d'eux est tellement unie
> A celle de Jesus (qui toutes choses peut)
> Qu'à sa grande bonté et clemence infinie
> Ils se conforment tous et veulent ce qu'il veult.
> (#105, f°. 36 verso)

XXIII. *Singerie*

This pamphlet, a conglomeration of prose and poetry, again covers the main social grievances of Artus Désiré. In part at least, it is based on his unpublished *Secret Conseil* to Charles IX, of which a number of passages have made their way into the *Singerie* more or less intact.

More striking, however, is its repetition of almost everything he had said since 1547: "paillardise" of women, corruption of judges and clergy, presumption of the new "theologians," and so forth. There is no purpose in another lengthy analysis; only a few points will be mentioned.

1. The *Secret Conseil* was written before the massacre of St. Bartholomew, and much of it was devoted to pleading for just such an extermination. The *Singerie* was published two years after the slaughter, which had not achieved its avowed purpose of eliminating heresy from France. It is this fact in part which led father Charbonnier to the conclusion that:

> les plus intransigeants parmi les adversaires de la Réforme, Artus Désiré entre autres, conseillaient maintenant au roi, non d'user de violence envers les dissidents, mais de réformer les mœurs dans la société ecclésiastique et civile...[1]

The fact is, as we have seen, that Désiré had consistently called for the correction of both clerical and civilian abuses, even in his earliest works; this is not, therefore, a new element in the *Singerie*. On the other hand, he did not in this work cease calling for another bloodbath, a fact recognized in mid 18th century by the bibilographer Gachet d'Artigniy, who noted in his description of this work that "... il ne tient pas à lui qu'on ne renouvelle la Saint Barthélemy. Il exhorte les Rois, les Princes et les Magistrats à faire massacrer tous les Calvinistes."[2] To cite only one example in refutation of Charbonnier:

---

[1] Charbonnier, p. 365.
[2] Gachet d'Artigny, p. 47.

> Or Sire, pour conclusion
> Si vous voulez apaiser Dieu
> Il les fault sans remission
> Brusler tous vifs à petit feu...
>
> (#108, f°. 37 verso)

Charbonnier, who cites only the Montaiglon edition of the *Singerie*, which consists only of the introductory poem, had perhaps not seen the complete text; it is clear, in any case, that his statement does not apply to Artus Désiré, who maintained the same violent and intransigeant position after the massacre as before.

2. There is an enlightening description of the process by which a whole diocese might be shifted from the religion of Rome to that of Geneva:

> ... Predicans et Ministres, tous Apostats et Moines reniez... qui ont jetté le froc aux orties, pour donner lieu à leur charnelle concupiscence, et autres povres gens mechaniques, qui ne sçavent Latin ne François, lesquels ont veu que noz Evesques et Prelats estoient occupez aux œuvres de la chair, et empeschez à faire la court aux dames, ayant trouvé leurs sieges vuydes et vacans, ils se sont mis dedans, et prins possession de leurs lieux et places, et de leur propre authorité se sont intronisez en la prelature...
>
> (#108, f°. 17 verso)

3. Like the "francs taulpins" in an earlier work, and the "chevaux de louage" later, the "marmots et guenons" play almost no role beyond their mention in the title. But there is one passage in the *Singerie*, which may serve to explain the title, and which also prefigures the "Catholicon" passage in the *Satire Ménippée*:

> En bref, c'est une beste fort ingenieuse et malicieuse que le singe, et pource les Bateleurs (qui ne sçavent rien de mentir) en font fort bien leur prouffit, par ce qu'elle est prompte et agile à donner plaisir et passe-temps à ceux qui la regardent. Donc ils la portent et pourmenent de ville en village par les foires et marchez, afin d'assembler, et attirer le menu peuple à leurs singeries et mensonges, pour vendre leurs faulses drogues esventées, qu'ils disent

> avoir apportées des pays estranges et lointaines regions, ce que font tout ainsi les bateleurs et triacleurs d'heresie, qui sont les predicans du diable d'enfer, lesquels s'en vont par pays avec leurs Guenons....
>
> (#108, f.º 11 recto)

4. Another argument foreshadows Bossuet's *Variations,* for Désiré asks of the Protestants in effect: By what authority do you claim to represent the truth? You are many small sects.

5. In the last few pages his warning of disaster becomes apocalyptic, as when he hurls this curse at the rich and powerful:

> Malheur sur vous (dict le prophete) qui vous estes veaustrez et couchez sur les grans tas de blé et tonneaux de vin, sans avoir pitié ne compassion de vos povres brebis, qui crient de faim et froit à la porte de voz chasteaux et palais, pour la necessité du pain, qui leur deffault, à vostre ruine et confusion...."
>
> (#108, f. 39 verso)

Again the evolution of his style is clear. His ideas are no longer presented according to an orderly plan, but are poured forth somewhat in the manner of an old testament prophet.

XXIV. *Ravage et deluge*

Désiré indicates the nature of this work in one of the opening paragraphs:

> Or pour entendre sainement ceste matiere et le subject de nostre discours, ces Chevaux de louage dont nous entendons parler, sont ces malheureux et miserables Diables deschanynez reistres, et souldartz de nostre païs de France, qui pour le jourd'huy precedent toutes nations en malice et cruauté, lesquels ne sçaurions mieux comparager qu'aux susdictz chevaux de louage, parce qu'ils sont de telle nature et a qui plus leur donne, gens sans loy, sans foy, sans congnoissance de Dieu, non plus que povres bestes bruttes, qui font grand marché de leurs corps et ames, qui donnent au Prince du monde pour peu de chose, comme Essau fist sa primogeniture à Jacob, pour une escullée de nantilles, les povres malheureux damnez cedent et quittent leur vie, part et portion de Paradis,

pour troys, ou quatre escus le moys, voire et se loüent au plus offrant et dernier encherisseur....

(#110, f°. 3 recto)

Lest his reader conclude that his epithet applies to soldiers on both sides, he makes it quite clear that the chevaux de louage are with the heretics: "... ces malheureux chevaux de louage.... ne veulent accorder ne confesser aucun libre arbitre, disant que ce que Dieu a predestiné est predestiné ou reprouvé, sans que personne puisse estre predestiné par oeuvres de vertus ne dignes fruictz de penitence." (#110, f°. 23 verso)

Aside from the heavy allegorical satire, which plays little part in the work, there is not much here which he has not already stated several times before. In this work, however, his grievances are stated with great force, and in greater detail than was sometimes the case. The result is a devastating picture of the nation, as seen by one of its more conservative commentators.

1) On the vanity of women's finery: After several pages of violent diatribe against the immorality of their clothes, he concludes "et pource, dites adieu à toutes vos Patenostres, Messes, Jeusnes et autres bienfaictz: Car tout cela n'est qu'autant de vent, si vous ne portez autres habitz plus modeste et honneste selon que vostre estat le requiert." (#110, f°. 21 verso)

2) Kings are responsible for the ills besetting the country; he urges them:

> ....recognoissez que si ladite justice eust eu lieu en vostre endroict comme au passé, que vos subjects et vassaulx, n'eussent eu la chair si hardie d'avoir prins les armes contre vous. Au temps de vos feux Peres Roys de France (que Dieu absolve) on ne voyoit par les grans chemins passans, et entrees de villes et bourgades que pendus, descapitez, esquartelez, brisez et rompus sur la roue, mais ce jourd'huy pas un. Combien que pour un mauvais garçon qui estoit en ce temps la, sont ce jourd'huy multipliez dix mille, ce qui cause.... la ruine du Royaume."

(#110, f°. 27 verso)

3) The same nostalgia for the "good old days" appears in regard to judges:

> .... aussi Messieurs les Magistratz et Juges criminelz, audict Royaume, depuis la mort du bon feu Roy Henry, un Royaume qui souloit estre le plus fameux et renommé....
>
> (#110, f°. 28 recto)

He explains the process by which corruption of the judiciary is accomplished:

> .... gardez vous bien ... de prester l'oreille ... aux Seigneurs et Dames qui bien souvent vous prient de soustenir le mauvais droict d'une partie, par le moyen de leur bonne grace et faveur.
>
> (#110, f°. 29 recto)

4) He has kind words and sympathy for the poor, victimized by usurers:

> Comme bien vous avez veu ces jours passez, de la famine et penurie des monnoyes, qui estoit tant grande, que si les povres gens vouloient avoir du pain, ilz estoient contrainctz l'acheter au quadruple, par les larrons usuriers, qui leur bailloient les pieces d'or à si hault pris, qu'ilz ne sçavoient autre chose que faire, sinon plorer auprès de leurs petis enfans qui mouroient de faim, chose qui doibt estre bien remarquée pour l'avenir. Car ce n'estoit faulte qu'il n'y en eust assez, mais la grande malice des usuriers et mauvais riches, qui affamoient tout le monde et desquelz l'avarice et usure fut si appertement descouverte, qu'il n'y eut jamais plus beau moyen de les recercher et punir corporellement qu'il y avoit alors, tesmoings les povres artisans qui eussent bien sceu dire, sont telz et telz, laquelle chose eust esté une grande purgation de vermine audict Royaume.
>
> (#110, f°. 28 recto-verso)

On the other hand, so as not to wander too far from his basic Catholic premises, he suggests that:

> .... esbahir ne se faut si Dieu retire la fertilité de la terre. Car au lieu de luy rendre les graces et dismes des biens qu'il nous donne, nous le blasphemons, et desrobons son droict de dismage qui c'est retenu des la creation du monde....
>
> (#110, f°. 30 verso)

He is fully as harsh in this work as anywhere towards the prelates and pastors of the Church, for the Protestants:

> prennent le fondement de leurs heresies, sur la mauvaise vie d'aucuns d'entre vous. Car le desordre et scandale y est tant grand, que si nostre Seigneur met la main dessus vous, il en fera une si terrible execution de vengeance qu'il vous vaudroit trop mieux... n'avoir onc esté nez....
> (#110, f°. 26 verso)

This time he makes a direct connection between the rich and the prelates, for he accuses the former of being the chief despoilers of the Church:

> encore plusieurs d'entre vous, qui par force et violence occupent et dissipent ceux de l'Eglise contre leurs propres consciences, sans aucun droict ne raison? Dictes hardiment que tous les docteurs theologiens et decretistes n'y entendent rien, si vous n'estes tous perdus ne damnez, si vous ne faictes penitence et restitution des lieux et places que vous tenez soubz le faux tiltre des coupeurs de lard de vos grasses cuisines, qui vous prestent leurs noms, sans aucune profession de l'estat ecclesiastique...
> (#110, f°. 31 verso-32 recto)

The *Ravage et deluge* concludes with a poem in which the crimes of the "chevaux" are detailed:

> Brusler les bleds.........
> ....jurer, blasphemer,
> ... ...
> Et faire au peuple tant d'outrage
> Que les povres gens de village
> Sont contrainctz de quitter leur terre.
>   Vendre et crier au plus offrant
> Le pucelage d'une fille....
> Faire payer deux ou trois mille
> Escus de rançon aux marchans,
> Destruire et raser tout aux champs....
>   Mettre le feu dans une Eglise
> Où tous les hommes du village
> S'estoient retirez en franchise
> Pour eviter vostre ravage
> Les faire brusler de grand rage

> Et rostir les prestres du lieu,
> Mettre tout à sang et à feu,
> Froisser les enfans comme un voirre,
> Lier les hommes deux à deux
> Pour faire vos œuvres lubriques,
> Et violer tout devant eux
> Leurs femmes et filles pudiques,
> Contraindre les povres rustiques
> Principalement les Chrestiens
> De racheter leurs propres biens
> Autour de la ville d'Auxerre...
>   Prendre les dessusdictes femmes
> Par force et les prostituer
> Comme des paillardes infames
> Et leurs batre et tuer, (sic)
> Desrober sans restituer
> Tous leurs biens jusques à la paille,
> Et contrainctz (pour payer la taille)
> Vendre leurs maisons et leur terre....
>
>   (#110, f°. 35 verso-36 recto)

Each eight and ten- line stanza concludes with "M'appelez vous cela la guerre?" or "Et que c'est usance de guerre?"

In a final burst Désiré urges the judges to be harsh in their sentences, for:

> Il n'est plus question d'user
> Envers eux de misericorde,
> Mais au lieu de les excuser
> Leur bailler une belle corde....
>
>   (#110, f°. 36 verso)

an ironic statement, since he had never from the beginning of his career recommended any other course.

XXIV. *Retour de Guillot*

The final message offered by Artus Désiré to his Catholic public was the *Retour de Guillot le Porcher,* published as a companion-piece to the *Ravage et deluge.* Guillot has returned to France after years of wandering, and of persecution by the heretics:

> ...pour une singerie
> Que j'ay faict imprimer contre leur diablerie,
> Et pour la cause aussi, d'une contrepoison
> Des chansons de Marot, en rime et sans raison,
> Dont ilz m'ont poursuivi plus de vingt ans y a,
> Mais la grace a mon Dieu encore me voila....
>
> Me voila revenu ancien et agé
> Non sans avoir beaucoup par les champs voyagé
> Mais tant veu de pais et respandre de sang
> Que mon poil grisonné, est devenu tout blanc.
>   (#110, f°. 37 verso)

Meeting the bergère again, whom he now addresses as Rauline, he describes to her his travels, and a series of dreadful visions of monsters and demons, who turn out to be .... the Huguenots. The two then engage in nostalgic reminiscences of the "good old days" of "deffunct Roy Henry," when France lived in peace and plenty:

Guillot: Et Rauline mamie, où est le temps passé
Qu'avions provision, de boisson, lard et pain...
Et ce jourd'huy mourons, quasi presque de faim?...
                              (#110, f°. 40 verso)

Bergère: Helas où est le temps qu'on en despeschoit tant,
Que quand un malfaicteur quelque cas commetoit,
Sans forme de procez, il estoit quant et quant
A mort executé, selon qu'il meritoit?
Par les chemins passans, Provinces et quartiers,
On les voioit pendus aux arbres haut et bas,
Les uns decapitez, les autres en quartiers
Qui faisoient grand horreur d'en voir tant en un tas....
                              (#110, f°. 42 verso)

There follows a long passage describing once again the ills besetting France, in which there is little of novelty: as usual the blame lies with women and their vanity and immorality; disobedient children; the corruption of the courts; immorality of the clergy, stemming from plurality of benefices. The following matters deserve mention:

1) An extensive discussion of economic woes, and a mention of the hardships endured by tenant farmers, indicating perhaps changes in land tenure and occupancy:

> Mais ce jourd'huy s'il faut un bail renouveler,
> Aux femmes faut donner (contre tout droict divin)
> La chaine d'or au col, pour danser et baller
> Et à monsieur cinquante ou cent escus de vin.
> Sans respecter en rien son service passé,
> Par l'avaricieux tenté de l'ennemy.
> Le povre homme sera de sa ferme chassé....
>
> (#110, f°. 41 recto-verso)

2) More open criticism of the government, and of the mignons (we are now well into the reign of Henri III):

> Mais quoy? ce sont mignons....
> Qui troussent leurs cheveux pour monstrer bon visage
> Avec de grans collectz d'un demy pied de large
> Tant bien chauderonnez (dy je dauderonnez)
> Que tous les Diables sont, à l'entour de leur nez
> A leur tortillonner leurs morveuses moustaches...
>
> (#110, f°. 50 verso)

> ....si on ne deffend la superfluité,
> Avant qu'il soit deux ans la multiplicité
> Des gros estats sera si difforme et infame,
> Que les libidineux prendront l'habit de femmes
> Et les femmes l'habit des hommes aveuglez....
>
> (#110, f°. 51 recto)

3) The poetic style of Artus Désiré: usually earthy or simply pedestrian, he was not given to excursions into the grand manner. However, in this work we encounter this astonishing tautology:

> Au matin que l'Aurore aube du point du jour
> Commenceoit à lever....
>
> (#110, f°. 43 verso)

4) Finally after striking a prophetic note, and predicting even more dire evidence of God's anger and punishment, Guillot propposes flight:

> Pource retirons nous hors de France nous deux
> Car la fureur de Dieu y est tant enflambée
> Que son ire divine est sur elle tombée....
>
> (#110, f°. 53 recto)

> Et veu qu'a tous propos on blaspheme son nom,
> Et que la foy du peuple est du tout corrompue
> Nous n'en sçaurions que dire, autre chose, sinon,
> Sauve soy qui pourra la Navire est rompue....
> (#110, f°. 55 recto)

His social views are of little more interest than his religious attitudes from which, of course, they stem. In fact, no matter how remote from the religious question some of his discussions may seem to be, we are always sooner or later shown that a connection exists.

His social opinions cover such a wide range, and are so inconsistent, that they are difficult to summarize. However, they center on certain recurrent themes, which he develops somewhat as follows:

1. France finds herself in a distressing condition: famine and pestilence are stalking the land and the nation is torn by internal conflicts.

2. The basic cause of all these evils is the Protestant heresy which has been making rapid headway among all classes of the population.

3. The heresy has at least three basic causes:

    a. The frustrated ambition of Martin Luther for the rank of cardinal.

    b. The desire on the part of apostate clergy to escape the laws of the church, especially that against marriage.

    c. The abuses within the church.

4. The poor example set for the public by the clergy has its source in the power of the king to make important clerical appointments. Benefices go to courtiers and their families, and this is the way in which heretics frequently make their way into important church positions.

5. The same is true for the magistrature. Positions are sold to the highest bidders, which again opens the way for heretics.

6. Once the church and the courts have been infiltrated, it is idle to expect the king and his government to correct the abuses, since they are responsible for them and would have to take measures against themselves.

7. This situation has led to a weakening of the moral fiber of the nation at all levels. Principal signs of laxity are:

   a. Lack of charity on the part of the rich towards the poor.

   b. Curiosity, vanity and profligacy of women. Inherently weak, and responsible for the original fall from grace, they are therefore more susceptible to the false teachings of the new religion.

   c. Upbringing of children. If they were raised properly and treated with the rigor they deserve, we would not have seen a whole generation grow up to reject the religion of their fathers.

   d. Widespread blasphemy, a cardinal sin itself.

   e. Ruinous monetary inflation, caused among other things by the dishonest practices of innkeepers.

Discounting the efficacy of his sermons to effect any significant reforms, we find that the solution he proposes for these evils has two facets:

1. The government, by a wiser selection of prelates and magistrates, can prevent new defections from the church.

2. To cope with the heretics and their sympathizers already among us, the only just remedy is immediate slaughter and burning.

CHAPTER IV

AN INÉDIT OF ARTUS DÉSIRÉ:
SECRET CONSEIL AU ROY CHARLES IX

Collection Rasse des Noeux, BN. ms Fr 22.561, ff 58v to 67r. Published with the permission of Bibliothèque Nationale in Paris.

The poem published here for the first time was written by Artus Désiré about 1568. It therefore signalizes a new and final burst of "literary" activity on his part, for no new work had been issued from his pen since 1561 or 1562, and this opuscule was to be followed by four others, before he finally lapsed into silence in 1578.

The presence of the word "secret" in the title has a real significance. It will be remembered that since 1561 Désiré had been officially in disgrace. After his attempt to enlist the active support of Philip II of Spain in behalf of the Catholic party in France, he had been condemned to five years imprisonment. His escape from confinement a few months later had not returned him to full royal favor, and in 1564 the king had ordered his banishment from the kingdom.

The present work perhaps represents an effort on his part to regain royal favor, without calling public attention to himself; he was able to give voice in it to some of his favorite phobias, and at the same time make use of the secrecy of its genesis to advocate directly to the king policies which he could never suggest in a more public document.

It would be surprising if Artus Désiré, who habitually pillaged his own published works, had not made use of this unpublished document in his later works. In fact, not only the ideas (few of which were new in any case) but also phrases and occasionally whole stanzas turned up almost intact, in the *Désordre et scandale,* in the *Origine et source de tous les maux,* and in the *Singerie des huguenots*. Some of the more obvious borrowings will be indicated at the appropriate place in this text.

What gives this manuscript a somewhat special interest is the fact that it was apparently never intended to be published, but was composed exclusively for the attention of the king. It is therefore unique among his works, in that it contains suggestions for policy changes which he might never have dared to broadcast in a public document.

For example, in no other work did he single out Catherine de Médicis for criticism; yet here he is bold enough to urge her retirement from public affairs. It is only in this little work that he expresses a wholly unfavorable opinion of Michel de l'Hôpital; and nowhere else was he so explicit in detailing just how some courtiers of Charles IX maintained relations with the rebellious Protestants even in time of war.

In addition there are differences of emphasis in this work, for example, his treatment of the clergy. In almost all his other writings, Désiré dwelt not only on the injustice with which appointments to high church offices were made, but also on the scandalous behavior of prelates and lowly monks alike. In the *Secret Conseil* this second consideration is totally ignored, except, by implication, as a biproduct of the first, which he dwelt upon at some length. The reason, of course, is that the king was in no position to influence directly the conduct of the clergy, whereas the nomination of prelates was his personal responsibility.

Again, in his other works he divided his attention between deploring the existing situation and making suggestions for improvement. In this poem, by its very nature, recommendations for improvement occupy much more space than descriptions of just how bad things are. Thus, from the beginning of his career he had proposed the burning of all heretics; but in this pamphlet he devotes a major part of his attention to their extermination, more than to almost any other single question.

The foregoing aspects of this little work give it a slightly different tone from anything else that he wrote. It moves faster, is less given to efforts at lofty eloquence, seems more personal and, somehow, more intense, Yet it shows most of the weaknesses of his other "literary" endeavors; it is badly organized and unwieldy in structure, trite and repetitive in expression, emphatic in style. More serious as defects, however, are the violence and ignorance of its conception, and the laxity and slovenliness of its composition. It cannot be taken seriously as literature.

The manuscript is dated "1568" at the beginning and at the end. There is no reason to question that this is the year in which it was delivered to the monarch, nor that it received its definitive form at that time. Yet there are several passages which seem to have been written earlier, even as early as 1564 or 1565.

"Tell the king," he says to his book, "Qu'ilz le feront encore enfant à plus de quatorze ans d'icy."

The inference from these lines is that the advisors of the king, by keeping from his hands effective control of the government, are maintaining his status as a child. As a rhetorical device it makes sense only if he was then 14 years old. "A plus de dix-huit ans d'icy" fits the meter exactly as well. It is reasonable to suppose, therefore, that these lines were written between June 1564 and June 1565, or shortly after the king was declared legally of age to rule.

Other lines suggest other dates prior to 1568:

1. "Un roy doibt à seize ans..." therefore, 1566-67.

2. "Jamais ne vivrés aage d'homme:" these words would certainly not be directed to a young monarch of 18, probably not at 16.

3. "Il feit un froid qui nous geloit, ...": "Désiré mentioned in the *Origine et source* that such a freeze took place in the winter of 1565, in much the same terms as here. Of course, the reference need not be to the winter just past.

None of these conflicting dates invalidate 1568 as probably the effective date of this *Conseil*. At most, they throw additional light on the carelessness with which he worked.

The page numbering of the Rasse des Noeux manuscripts is erratic. In fact there are three series of page or folio numbers covering the pages of the *Secret Conseil*.

The title and opening lines of text appear verso of folio 58 according to one set. But this page is designated 40 in the upper left corner. At the bottom of this page is ... [58]

The second page of text gives in the upper right corner folio 59, with page 41, and at the bottom ... [59]

These three series of numbers then continue through the 19 pages of text. Thus the next to last page is indicated upper right as folio 67, page 57; at the bottom of the page as [75].

The final page is verso folio 67 and has no numbers at the top. At the bottom is number [78], which is clearly in error.

In the following pages I have used the folio numbers of the upper right corner, starting with number 58Vo and ending with 67Vo, since these are the most regular and consistent.

The text is presented substantially as it appears in the manuscript. Archaisms and most inconsistencies in spelling have been left intact. There are, however, obvious errors in transcription, and these have been corrected in the text, with a notation of the manuscript reading beside the line. In addition, I have separated words run together; added apostrophes and acute accents when necessary for the sense; spelled out abbreviations, such as *vre*, *nre*, using standard 16th century orthography *vostre*, *nostre*; and added punctuation for clarity. Explanatory notes, cross references to other works, and all other commentary will be found in footnotes at the bottom of each page.

Secret Conseil

f. 58Vo

Suz la refformation des Abus de ce royaume
Fait Par Mess. Artus Désiré Prestre: au
Nom des Caillettes Catholicques Badaux de
Paris addressé au Roy Charles IX. 1568.

Mon livre qui selon DIEU parles
  De la Verité librement
  Va te presenter au Roy Charles
  En son Palais secretement
  Marche et despesche vistement

Et dy que c'est moy qui t'envoye   Ms. l'envoye
Mais que je luy prie humblement
Quil n'y ait que luy qui te voye [1]

Tu luy diras aussy qu'il fault
  Qu'il nous gouverne ce jourdhuy,
  Parce que l'entendement fault
  A ceux qui gouvernent soubz luy,
  Et que s'il n'est craint et ouy
  Autant du petit que du grand,
  Que ceux de son conseil errant
  Luy causeront tant de soulcy
  Qu'ilz le feront encore enfant
  A plus de quatorze ans d'icy [2]

Or va, Dieu te veulle conduire,
  Et donner grace que sans moy
  Tu puisses bien hardiment dire
  Ce qui est contenu en toy.
  Car s'il faict cela, jamais Roy   f. 59Ro
  Ne fut de tel bruit et renom,
  Qu'il exaltera hault son nom,
  Et ses ennemis raliez
  Seront mis par nom et surnom
  Soubz la scabelle de ses piedz. [3]

   Au Roy Charles neufiesme de ce nom,
       Artus Désiré, le moindre de
         ses treshumbles orateurs,
             grace et perpetuelle
                 felicité.

Souverain Prince Treschrestien,
  Par grace de dieu Roy de France,
  Nous vous supplions prendre bien
  Ce petit livre d'importance,
  Qui vous remonstre l'abondance

---

[1] It is evident from the text that this desire to be read only by the king, or by those designated by him, was genuine. This is not a public document.

[2] These two lines make best sense if the king was fourteen years old when they were written. This would place the date of composition of these lines between June 1564 and June 1565. It does not follow, however, that the poem was completed and delivered at that time; all that it indicates is that Artus Désiré had conceived and begun to execute his project several years before 1568.

[3] "So that he will exalt his name, and his ennemies who have rallied againts him will be ranged by name and surname beneath.... his feet."

Des pechez regnanz faulsement;
Desquelz n'avez pas congnoissance
Faulte d'un advertissement.

Aux grandz clameurs et doleances
  De vos subjetz qui destruictz sont,
Nous vous faisons les remonstrances
  De plusieurs abus qui se font.
Et pour ceste occasion, Sire,
  Supplions vostre humanité
Vous regler dessus nostre dire,
  Qui ne contient que verité.

Nous disons, pour commencement,
  Que si voullez que paix ait lieu,
Qu'il fault cercher premierement
  Tous les moiens d'appaiser DIEU.

f. 59Vo

Et secondement, qu'on punisse
  Tout vice et peché qui abonde;
Car un Roy qui est sans justice
  Ne peult regner longtemps au monde.

Et pour ce faire il fault avoir
  De bons prelatz en prelature,
Et gens de bien et de scavoir
  Es sieges de judicature. [4]

Car vous voyez appertement
  Que l'ire de DIEU est tombée
Sur nous universellement
  Par vostre justice courbée.

Sy les grandz faultes et trespas
  Eussiez faict punis par arrest,
Vostre royaulme ne fût pas
  Perdu et destruict comme il est;

Et faire mourir les mauvais [5]
  Qui ce jourdhuy vous font la guerre,
Vous nous eussiez mis en grand paix
  Et faict trembler toute la terre.

---

[4] These are two of the commonest complaints of Désiré.

[5] The structure of the sentence is: "Si vous eussiez fait punir... (et que vous eussiez fait) faire mourir les mauvais...."

DIEU l'avoit ainsy ordonné,
   Et pource aigrement vous reprend;
   Car vous leur avez pardonné,
   Dont voyez comme il vous en prent.

La punition qu'il nous donne
   Provient de vostre faulte et tort,
   Car il ne veult point qu'on pardonne
   A ceulx qui sont dignes de mort. [6]

Tesmoing l'antien testament,
   Qui dict que plusieurs pechans
   Ont esté puniz grevement
   Pour avoir faict grace aux meschans:

f. 60Ro

Et pource que Saül feit grace
   Au roy Achab, fier et cruel,
   Un berger feut mis en sa place
   Et couronné roy d'Israël. [7]

Il les fault doncque, pour la foy,
   Punir, sans les laisser courir,
   Ou bien que ne soiez plus roy
   Et qu'ilz nous facent tous mourir;

Ce qu'ilz feront si DIEU n'y met
   Ordre bien tost, et si pour vous
   A la commune on ne permet
   De leur couper la gorge à tous.

Pource, Seigneur, donnez puissance
   A tout vostre peuple commun
   De vous en faire la vengeance, [8]
   Car ilz sont cent hommes contre un. [9]

Et faites par commandement
   Desborder tous voz platz pais,
   Et vous verrez en un moment
   Les chiens matins bien esbahis.

---

   [6] Cf. *Singerie:*   Car Dieu ne veult point qu'on pardonne
                       A ceux qui sont dignes de mort....
followed by the same examples.
   [7] The same reference to Saul and Achab occurs likewise in the *Origine et source de tous les maux.*
   [8] This bit of advice in 1568 exactly prefigures the massacre of 1572.
   [9] Presumably the meaning here is that *we* outnumber *them* 100 to 1.

Mais il fault necessairement,
   Avant toute œuvre par raison,
   Faire mourir premierement
   Les traistres de vostre maison.

Car tant que vous en souffrirez
   Un seul ou seulle aupres de vous,
   De plus en plus provocquerez
   La fureur de DIEU contre nous [10]   Ms. faveur

He, Seigneur! ne voyez-vous point
   Qu'ils jouent de vous à la paulme,
   Et en quel ordre et piteux point
   Ont mis vostre pauvre royaume?
                                           f. 60Vo

Vous estes trahy et vendu
   Comme la chair devant le stal,
   Et tout vostre peuple perdu
   Pour un belistre d'Hospital. [11]   Ms. d'hospital

Non pas pour luy tant seulement
   Mais d'aultres qu'estimez amis,
   Qui tendent ordinairement
   A vous livrer aux ennemis.

Les trois partz de vos domesticques
   Tant officiers que conseillers
   Sont parfaictz meschantz hereticques, [12]
   Et vos plus grands familiers. [13]   Ms. Et vous

Il fault doncq de vostre maison
   Chasser hors tous les malheureux,
   Ou bien par justice et raison
   Que Dieu vous punisse pour eux.

Car indubitablement, Sire,
   Si à un seul faictes mercy,

---

[10] Cf. *Singerie:*   Tant que vous en souffrirez un
                       Pres de vous ne en autre lieu,
                       C'est un final arrest commun
                       Que vous n'aurez la paix de Dieu.

[11] Michel de l'Hospital. Jodelle also singled him out for special attack.

[12] "Within your own household the numerical alignment is 3 to 1 against you."

[13] For best sense, this line should be read before the preceding line.

Dessus vous respandra son ire   Ms. respendra
Et sur nous tous aultres aussy.[14]

Et comme seroit-il possible
  De rendre par les gens de bien
Nostre dict royaulme paisible   Nostre... royaulme,
  Quand vostre conseil ne vault rien?[15] ms. not clear

Vous ne scauriez avoir ouvert
  Si tost la bouche à l'un d'entr'eux
Que le tout ne soit descouvert
  A voz ennemis malheureux.

Et pour ceste occasion, Sire,
  Vous les devriez tous sequestrer
De vostre conseil, et leur dire
  Qu'ilz n'ayent plus à y entrer.
                                           f. 61Ro

Le diable d'enfer les tient là
  Enchaynez sans repos ne somme,
Et si vous ne chassez cela
  Jamais n'y vivrés aage d'homme.[16]

Car ilz vous portent tel envie
  Contre DIEU et contre raison
Qu'à la fin auront vostre vie
  Par glaive ou mortelle poison.

Voire, si vous n'y donnez ordre,
  Avant que la poison soit meure;
Car si grand y est le desordre
  Que tout vostre peuple en murmure.

Vostre medecin ne vault rien;
  Vostre appoticquaire encor moins;
Non faict vostre chirurgien;
  Et pource ostez-vous de leurs mains.

---

[14] Cf. *Singerie:* Car pour certain asseurons nous
                    Que si nous pardonons au moindre
                    Dieu nous exterminera tous....

[15] This whole section is evidence that the document was intended for the king's eyes only. In his published works he never pointed his finger so clearly at the king's associates, probably because he could not know who would read them.

[16] Another indication that Charles IX was still probably less than 18.

Bien mieux vaudroit au temps qui court
  Prendre conseil de voz marchans
  Que d'un tas de paillardz meschans
  Que vous tenez en vostre court.

Et pource, Sire, commencez
  A faire justice regner,
  Sans vous laisser plus gouverner
  Par gens charnelz et insensez.   Ms. incensez

Et ne declarez vos affaires
  A plusieurs qu'estimez des vostres,
  Parce qu'ilz sont cousins et freres
  De voz ennemiz et des nostres. [17]

Car au rapport de gens scavantz,
  Un roy doibt à seize ans avoir [18]
  Plus de prudence et de scavoir
  Qu'un aultre homme à quatrevingtz ans.
                                                        f. 61Vo

Un malade est en mauvais point
  Et en grand danger de sa vie
  Quand par conseil il ne veult point
  Desraciner sa maladie.

Ainsy que vous avez permis
  En vostre royaulme deux loix,
  Nostre Seigneur Dieu vous a mis
  Pour retribution deux roys. [19]

---

[17] Cf. *Singerie:*   Faictes punition nouvelle
                       Sans en parler à leurs amis;
                       Car la chair et le sang revelle
                       Vos secrets à vos ennemis....

[18] Still another indication that the king was less than 18.

[19] These lines are not clear. Apparently they mean that "just as you have allowed on your territory another religion to vie with Catholicism, so the leader of that sect can be considered a rival of yourself. In 1568, however, there was no real threat of a rival temporal leader.

    Cf. *Singerie:*
            Car tant que permettrez deux loix
            Soyez certains qu'aurez tousjours
            En France deux Dieux et deux Roys....

    Cf. also, *Desordre et scandale:*
           Nous avons double loy, double foy, double eglise,
            Doubles opinions de conseil variable
            Double parole au cueur qui fort nous scandalise,
            Deux en un lict couchez, l'un à Dieu, l'autre au diable.

O Seigneur experimenté,
  Treschrestien entre meschans gens,
  Et que vous estes tourmenté
  Et soufflé de malheureux vens!

Mais prenez-le bien et scachez
  Que ceste terrible escarmouche
  Est la main de Dieu qui vous touche
  Pour les offenses et pechez.

Et si vous estes mol et vain
  A faire mourir les mauvais,
  Asseurez-vous pour tout certain
  Que jamais ne serez en paix.

Vous devez comme un Pelican
  Desirer mourir pour les vostres
  Sans vous fier à vostre camp,
  Car plusieurs sont d'avec les aultres.

Cela est tout clair et commun
  Que tous les deux n'ont qu'une nappe;
  Et avez dix hommes contre un,
  Et si au diable l'un qui frappe [20]

Parquoy il fault bien dire, Sire,
  Qu'ilz [21] ont commendement expres
  De ne leur mesfaire ou mesdire,
  Ne de les poursuivre de pres,

f. 62Ro

Ce qui se faict pour les laisser
  Par un conseil traistre et mauvais, [22]
  Affin de vostre camp casser
  Pour vous contraindre à faire paix.

Car si, selon nostre souhait,
  On eust permis à tous ceux-là
  De frapper depuis qu'ils sont là
  Longtemps y a que ce fut faict.

Ms. qui sont la
Ms. Longtemps y que

---

[20] Not clear. Perhaps the meaning is that "some in your camp are in league with the enemy. But you outnumber the traitors 10 to 1; therefore do not hesitate to strike first.

[21] "those faithful to you."

[22] "This is done to keep them under traitorous and evil orders."

Mais tous les jours on les retarde,
   Pour vous causer de grandz courroux
   Pource (Seigneur) donnez-vous garde
   De ceux qui sont aupres de vous.

Gideon, homme de bon sens,
   Hardy, courageux et habille,
   N'ayant des hommes que trois cens,
   On tua six vingtz quinze mille.

Et si vous aviez comme luy
   Gendarmes devotz et humains,
   Asseurez-vous que cejourdhuy
   DIEU ne vous en feroit pas moings.

Mais au lieu d'hommes Catholicques,
   Vous avez quasi les trois partz [23]
   De voz gendarmes hereticques,
   Qui pis sont que larrons pendartz.

Pensés-vous, Prince vertueux,
   Que DIEU ayde à telle canaille,
   Quant il ne fault que l'un d'entre eux
   Pour faire perdre une bataille.

Non, non, mais souvien au contraire,
   Il permet tenir une guerre
   Pour les saccager et desfaire,
   Affin d'en delivrer la terre,

f. 62Vo

Et pour nous corriger aussy
   D'une infinité de pechez
   Qui nous ont causé tout cecy,
   Dont sommes grandement fachez.

Aussy à la verité, Sire,
   Lesdictz pechez estoient et sont
   Si tresgrandz qu'on ne scauroit dire
   Les meschancetez qui se font.

Principalement à l'eglise
   Il y avoit et encore a
   Tant d'abus d'orgueil et feintise
   Que DIEU s'est faché de cela. [24]

---

[23] The ratio again seems to be three to one against the king.

[24] In this and following stanzas, he returns to one of his favorite topics, venality and corruption in the granting of church benefices.

Voz deffunctz peres negligens
   Y ont mis tant de meschans hommes
   Et tant de malheureuses gens
   Que vous voyez où nous en sommes.

Contre tous droictz et privileges
   Y ont esleu des malheureux
   Simoniacles, Sacrileges,
   Que vous continuez comme eux.

Helas! Sire roy, s'ilz pouvoient
   Parler à vous en chambres closes,
   Vray dieu, helas! qu'ilz vous diroient
   De grandz et merveilleuses choses.

Et pource pensez à cela,
   Car ce n'est pas petit peché
   Que de donner à ces gens là
   Une abbaye ou Evesché.

Autant faictes-vous des offices,
   Dont chacun se contriste moult,
   Car à nourrir tousjours les vices
   Jamais n'y aura fin ne bout.

f. 63Ro

Et pource (Seigneur) presentez
   Gens vertueux et de scavoir,
   Car à faire ainsy, vous mettez
   Tout vostre peuple en desespoir.

Et si vous n'usez de rigueur
   Contre la malice des grands,
   Soyez tout asseuré, Seigneur,
   Que jamais ne vivrez deux ans. [25]

Mes cinq sens sont si fort esmeuz
   De vous veoir en un tel danger
   Que si j'estois Nostredamus,
   Je n'en scaurois plus presager.

Doncq affin que le sang s'estanche,
   Monstrez-vous homme triumphant,
   Et que vous n'estes plus enfant
   Pour vous moucher à vostre manche.

---

[25] Désiré here suggests that if Charles IX does not "user de rigueur," he will not survive two years; it is interesting to note that when he did "user de rigueur" in 1572, he survived exactly two years.

Portez l'armure et le heaulme
   Dessus vostre dos, et au lieu
   De quereller vostre royaulme,
Querellez la cause de dieu.

Punissez les deffectueux
   Qui ont destruict et gasté tout,
   Car si vous n'estes vertueux
Jamais vous n'en viendrez à bout.

Bruslez les ordures infames
   Qui causent la perdition
   De cinq cens mille povres ames [26]   Ms. De cinq cens
Qui tombent en dampnation.   mil ames

Faictes les grevement punir
   Tant que la poudre en volle en l'air,
   Affin qu'au temps à l'advenir
Le feu n'y trouve que brusler.

                                                           f. 63Vo

Et si apres quelcun restoit,
   Faictes le punir promptement,
   Sans pardonner aucunement
A vostre bras s'il s'en sentoit.

Ilz sont de si mauvaise vie
   Et pleins d'execrables blasphemes
   Que tout vostre peuple vous prie
De ne vous fier qu'à vous mesmes.

Vous permettez à ceux qui sont
   Demourez, vivre parmy nous
   Soubz pretexte et couleur qu'ilz n'ont
Porté les armes contre vous.

Et si ceux qui tiennent les champs,
   A tout mal faire abandonnez,
   Rencontroient quelques bons marchans,
Ilz sont tuez ou rençonnez.

Et les faulx traistres inhumains,
   Que souffrez sans estre reprins,
   Ne doibvent-ilz point pour le moins
Recompenser ceux qui sont prins?

---

[26] *Singerie* contains the precise line "De cinq cens mille povres ames."

Ouÿ bien, mais vous ne voullez,
   Et par les traistres bien venuz
   Voz pauvres subjectz sont foullez
   Et voz ennemiz soustenuz.

Ceux que souffrez par injustice,
   Autant les grandz que les petitz,
   Vous portent plus de prejudice
   Que les meschans qui sont sortiz.

Car tous les jours les advertissent
   De voz deliberations,
   Et de deniers ilz en fournissent
   Pour avoir admonitions.[27]

f. 64Ro

Doncq, Seigneur, monstrez que vous estes
   Vray deffenseur de la foy vive,
   Car à faire ainsy que vous faictes
   Jamais n'y aura fondz ne rive

Ne voyez-vous qu'on vous trahit,
   Veu que jamais roy terrien
   N'eut tant de gens sans faire rien
   Qu'avez, dont chacun s'esbahit.

Mais mieux vaudroit n'avoir que deux
   Ou trois cens hommes Catholicques,
   Que cinq cens hommes malheureux
   Telz que sont noz larrons publicques.

O que de volleurs respanduz
   En ce royaulme douloureux!
   Et que de pauvres gens perduz
   Par vostre conseil malheureux!

Que de regretz souspirs et pleurs!
   Que de pauvreté et malheurs!
   Et que d'eglises magnificques
   Destruictes par voz domesticques!

Helas! Seigneur, si vous voyez
   Les grands maulx que font voz gendarmes   Ms. grand
   A voz pauvres subjects, croyez   Ms. subjectz croyez
   Que fondriez en pleurs et larmes.

---

[27] Those who have remained advise those who have left of your plans, and the latter pay for this information.

Brief l'ire de DIEU est tombée
  Sur vostre couronne et heaulme,
Et sa fureur si emflambée
  Qu'il vault myeux quitter le royaulme;

Car toute la terre est maudite
  Par la prevarication
De vostre maison interdite,
  Pleine d'abomination.

                                          f. 64Vo

A jamais vous serez coulpable
  Des doulleurs où tombez nous sommes,
Car vous n'estes plus excusable
  Devant DIEU ne devant les hommes.

Nostre maladie est si grande
  Et sommes en si mauvais point
Que pour l'edit que DIEU commande   Ms. ledit
  Nul de nous ne s'amende point.

Tous les jours on nous faict la paix,
  Tous les jours on nous faict la guerre, [28]
Par les volleurs traistres suspectz
  Qui troublent le ciel et la terre.

Mais croyez pour certain, Seigneur,
  Que tous ceux qui en [29] ont envye
Sont grandement suspectz d'erreur,
  Et qu'ilz n'ayment pas vostre vie.

Car la paix qu'on vous brasse et forge
  Est pour se raprocher de vous,
Affin de vous couper la gorge
  Et de nous exterminer tous. [30]

Ce qu'ilz feront sans fiction
  Si ladicte paix on leur donne,
Car toute leur intention
  Est d'usurper vostre couronne.

---

[28] Meaning not clear. Perhaps: "They *propose* peace, but make war."
[29] for peace.
[30] Cf. *Singerie:*   Leur paix est une paix de terre,
               Une paix de sedition
               Une paix de dampnation
               Une paix de traistres infames...
His warning is much more specific in the *Secret conseil*.

Ce sera tousjours à reffaire,
  Et jamais elle n'aura lieu,
  Car telle paix ne se peult faire
  Sans avoir guerre contre DIEU. [31]

Et pource gardez-vous en bien,
  D'aultant que vous aymez à vivre;
  Et par l'advis de gens de bien
  Suivez le conseil de ce livre.

f. 65Ro

Car quand ladite paix feriez,
  Elle ne seroit recepvable
  Pour autant que vous ne scauriez
  Accorder DIEU avec le diable.

Doncques il fault exterminer
  Leur camp qui voz villes despeuple,
  Car vous ne pouvez pardonner
  L'interest de DIEU et du peuple.

Pour accorder et satisfaire
  A toutes noz humbles requestes,
  Las! y auroit-il tant affaire
  A couper trois ou quatres testes?

Et nenny! de par DIEU, nenny!
  Mais vostre conseil par trop doux,
  D'heresie et d'erreur honny,
  Estoit plus pour eux que pour vous.

Voila, Seigneur, ce qui nous tient
  En trouble et guerre qui abonde,
  Et la racine d'où provient
  Toute la malice du monde.

Vous estes le speculateur,
  Qui rendrez compte en temps et lieu
  Du meschant et mauvais pasteur
  Que mettez au temple de DIEU.

Et si vous voullez prosperer,
  Mettez gens de bien aux offices,
  Et gardez bien de conferer
  Aux malheureux les benefices.

---

[31] These lines bring out clearly the intransigeance of the ultra Catholic party.

Es dignitez de prelature
  Constituez tous gens de bien,
  Et en vostre judicature
  Bons juges, sans en prendre rien. [32]

Jamais Pharao l'orgueilleux,
  Enflé de rage et de courroux,
  N'eust tant de signes merveilleux
  Ne d'advertissement que vous.

                                      f. 65Vo

Pour premiere admonition,
  DIEU nous osta vostre feu pere,
  Et apres par punition
  Le roy Françoys vostre bon frere.

Et pour seconde affliction,
  Vous ordonna jeune enfant roy,
  Dont le royaulme en tuition
  Fut mis à nostre grand esmoy [33]

Car aussy tost les troubles veindrent,
  Avec famine, peste et guerre,
  Et les larrons qui noz biens prindrent,
  Tant que pitié fut sur la terre.

DIEU voyant que nul ne voulloit
  S'amender dehors ne dedans,
  Il feit un froid qui nous geloit
  Le pain de bouche entre les dens. [34]

Vignes et noyers mesmement
  Feurent gelées de telle sorte
  Que la racine seche et morte
  Ne produit raisin ne sarment.   Ms. serment

Et lorsque noz traistres meschans
  Estoient en conseil ensemblez,
  Si grandz ventz furent par les champs
  Qu'ilz egrenerent tous les bledz.

---

[32] Without accepting money, in other words, put an end to "la vénalité des charges."

[33] Not a tactful remark. Cf. *Origine et source*: "... car une des plus grandes punitions qu'il puisse envoyer à un peuple c'est luy donner un jeune enfant pour roy."

[34] This deep freeze was mentioned in *Origine et source de tous les maux* as occurring in the winter of 1565. This date has no bearing on the date of composition of this document, since he need not have mentioned the event until much later.

Et cela presageoit-il point
  Ceste guerre et affliction,
Et que nous estions sur le point
  De plus grand tribulation.

Ouÿ veritablement, Sire,
  Au souverain rapport de tous,   Ms. de vous
Dont il nous fault conclure et dire
  Qu'il est fort faché contre nous.

Et pour appaiser sa fureur,
  Il fault que justice soit faicte
Des meschans qui sont faux envieux,
  Dont vostre maison est infaicte.
                                    f. 66Ro

Car c'est un arrest tout commung
  Que jamais n'aurez paix prospere
Tant que vous en souffriez ung,
  Et feust-il vostre propre pere.

Doncques, affin que vous puissiez
  Regner sur nous et nous soubz vous,
Tous noz ennemis punissez,
  Et alors DIEU sera pour vous.

C'est à ceste heure ou bien jamais
  Que devriez d'un cœur triumphant
Les debeller sans faire paix,
  Parce que n'estes plus enfant.

Non Seigneur (au rapport de tous)
  Pour estre gouverné d'aultruy,
Mais au contraire c'est à vous
  A vous gouverner ce jourdhuy.

Gouvernez-nous doncques, affin
  Que par vostre bon jugement
Nous puissions bien tost voir la fin
  De ce terrible advenement.

Ordonnez quelque bonne chose
  Pour estancher le sang caillé,
Et que Madame se repose,
  Car ell'a beaucoup travaillé [35]

---

[35] Another tactless remark, if this ms. were ever intended to be made public. This bit of advice occurs nowhere in his published works. What he is suggesting here is a coup d'état, in which the king would seize real power from his mother.

Faictes-nous ce grand bien pour elle,
　De prendre sa place et son lieu,
　Affin que plus ell'ne se mesle
De rien sinon servir à DIEU.

Elle a porté tant de tourmentz　　　　　　Ms. Elle à
　Par ceux qui ont sur elle envie
　Que tout le monde seurement
S'esbahit comme elle est en vie.

Et pource vous ferez tres bien
　De voz affaires disposer,
　Et de la laisser reposer
Sans s'entremesler plus de rien.　　　　　Ms. S'en s'entre-
　　　　　　　　　　　　　　　　　　　　　　mesler

Car il n'appartient nullement　　　　　　f. 66Vo
　(Sans fouller l'honneur de Madame)
　De bailler le gouvernement
D'un tel royaume à une femme. [36]

Par faulte d'avoir rencontré
　Au lieu d'elle un vertueux homme,
　Vous voyez appertement comme
Vostre royaulme est accoustré.

Doncq comme roy bien entendu
　Usez d'auctorité supreme,
　Car pour cest an tout est perdu
Si vous ne gouvernez vous-mesme.

Faict ou failly ou rien qui vaille, [37]
　Procedez vertueusement
　A faire donner la bataille,
Sans y languir si longuement.

Voire aussy, commandant à tous
　Les postes qui seront en voye
　Ne donner ad'aultres qu'à vous
Les pacquetz que l'on vous envoye.　　　Ms. que lon

---

[36] Désiré's low regard for women was based directly on his theology: the primary guilt of Eve for Original Sin and the fall from grace.

[37] Fairly clear reading, but the meaning is not exactly clear; perhaps: "Whatever you may do, whether successor failure, if it is to have any value proceed virtuously...."

Toutes personnes s'esbahissent   Ms. esbahissent
  Comme declarez voz affaires
  Aux parens de voz adversaires,
  Car ce sont ceulx qui vous trahissent. [38]   Ms. trahisent

Et pour ceste cause et raison
  Qu'ilz sont suspectz en la matiere,
  Ilz doibvent par loy coustumiere
  Se retirer en leur maison.

Ostez les doncq comme suspectz,
  Pour eviter murmure et blasme;
  Aultrement jamais n'aurez paix
  Ne repos au cœur de vostre ame.
                                   f. 67Ro

Nous portons aussy grand ennuy
  De plusieurs qui ne vallent rien,
  Que Monsieur tient aupres de luy
  Comme s'ilz estoient gens de bien.

Car le diable les y a mis   Ms. les y à
  Pour user de quelque surprise,
  Et pour dire à voz ennemis
  Tous voz secretz et entreprises.

Et pource mettez en leur lieu
  Des hommes vertueux et bons,
  Ou bien que vous et nous tombions
  En la main du glaive de DIEU.

Outre cela, faictes les tous
  Brusler comme fagotz de paille, [39]
  Car tant qu'ilz seront pres de vous,
  Jamais ne ferez rien qui vaille.

Et ainsy qu'un vertueux roy,
  Faictes l'edict et ordonnance   Ms. ledict
  Qui serve à vos subjectz de loy
  Par tout le royaulme de France.

C'est que tous enfans hereticques
  Ne puissent nulz bien heriter,
  Et que les peres Catholicques
  Les puissent tous desheriter.

---

[38] If he has specific individuals in mind, there is no indication of exactly whom.

[39] Cf. *Singerie:* Il les fault sans remission
                Brusler tous vifs à petit feu....

Cela les tiendra tous en crainte,
   Et seront contrainctz de par vous
   Obeyr à l'eglise saincte
   Et de vivre ainsy comme nous. [40]

Et au surplus, de voz chasteaulx
   Nettoyez les chambres et salles
   D'un tas de gros villains maraulx,
   Qui sont devant DIEU ors et salles.

                                              f. 67Vo

Ou aultrement, come dict est,
   Jamais vous ne prospererez.
   Et pource, Seigneur, s'il vous plaist,
   Plus de temps ne differerez.

Deliberez-vous d'un cœur franc,
   Sans aucune crainte ne doubte,
   Respandre pour DIEU vostre sang
   Jusques à la derniere goutte.

Vous et nos deux Seigneurs voz freres,
   Disposez en secret si bien
   De voz affaires necessaires,
   Que les meschans n'en sachent rien.

Et que foy soit en vous congneue, [41]   Ms. *sic*
   En considerant en tout lieu
   Que n'estes tous qu'une poignée
   De poudre et cendre devant DIEU.

Voila, Seigneur, le contenu
   De ce petit livre present,
   Duquel vostre peuple menu
   Vous faict remonstrance et present.

---

[40] Désiré never seems to have been able to understand that some people were willing to make any sacrifice, of property or even of their lives, for their convictions. His own abject plea for mercy in 1561 perhaps explains why he expected so little heroism from others.

[41] This faulty rhyme is nevertheless a clear reading in the Ms.

   Cf. *Singerie:*   Que la foy soit en vous cognée
                      Et reconnaissez en tout lieu
                      Que n'estes tous qu'une poignée
                      De pouldre et cendre devant Dieu....

Le tout est pour vous advertir,
 De peur que n'y laissiez le gaige;
 Car c'est un trop tard repentir
 Quand il fault trousser le bagaige. [42]

   Fin

   1568

---

[42] Cf. *Desordre et scandale:*
   Et pource soyons promps et tous prests de partir
   Quand Dieu nous mandera peur d'y laisser le gage,
   Car finablement c'est trop tard se repentir
   Quand il fault s'en aller et trousser le bagage.

This stanza is a good measure of the general laxity of his style, for in the alexandrines, with fifty per cent more space, he has added nothing to the content of the octosyllabic stanza.

CONCLUSION

We have now reviewed both the known facts in the life of Artus Désiré, and what little else has been said about him. We have listed editions of those works he is known to have written and a few others sometimes attributed to him. We have analyzed most of his works to show his principal preoccupations and how he dealt with them. And we have presented the text of a previously unpublished poem of some 600 lines to show the narrowness of his intellectual range and the lengths to which he was willing to go to achieve his violent ends.

If it is a truism to say that all artists reflect the time and place in which they create their work, it is equally true that they need not react artistically to each event in the world around them. Désiré was a child of his times. Yet there is little in his work to indicate a personal reaction to specific events.

He spanned in his literary career, 1545 to 1578, all or part of five different reigns. He witnessed, therefore, a number of changes in royal policy towards the religious problem in France. Under Francis I he was probably already engaged in his functions as priest at the time of the *Affaire des Placards* in 1534. To judge from his known published works, he began his literary efforts about ten years later, while France still suffered from the repression which characterized the last years of the reign of Francis I. But, if one were to believe Désiré, nothing had yet been done to stamp out the heresy then gaining ground among a large percentage of the population.

The reign of Henry II (1547-1559), with its regrouping of political forces, and its preoccupation with external affairs as well as the religious question, brought no change in the intransigeant attitude of Artus Désiré. On the contrary, he redoubled his efforts to eliminate the heretics. In the same way, under Francis II and the regency of Catherine de Médicis, there was no measurable diminution of his violence; it required the *Colloque de Poissy* of 1561 with its vague threat of an understanding between the opposing Catholic and Huguenot forces, to send Désiré on his ill-fated journed to demand of Philip II of Spain his intervention in the affairs of France.

Undaunted by the failure of his misison, Désiré next tried to exert an influence directly on Charles IX through his *Secret Conseil* of 1568. Here his efforts were directed to provoking precisely that bloody encounter which was to take place four years later in the St. Barthélémy Massacre. Yet from the beginning of his career he had never sought anything else; and far from being appeased by the slaughter of 1572, he continued after that date and until the end of his life to demand another and more thorough purge of heretics and of those who might conceivably be presumed such, just as though the *Massacre* had never taken place.

It would be inaccurate, therefore, to speak of a development of his thought. His position never changed. One could, perhaps, speak of some slight adaptation to changing circumstances. Yet, even here, Désiré can serve only remotely as guide to the evolving conditions in France. It is true, for example, that Martin Luther was the first major figure to threaten a split in the Church of Rome, and that Désiré chose Luther as his first specific target for criticism among the "Luthériens" in 1546-47. But long before that date, Calvin had founded his Church in Geneva. Yet Calvin did not appear as the chief villain in Désiré's works until about 1558.

Clément Marot was another of the dissidents who obsessed Artus Désiré. Marot had died in 1542 before Désiré had even begun to publish, yet our poet continued to fulminate against his translations of the *Psalms* until very late in his career. Finally, although Théodore de Bèze succeeded to the leadership of the Calvinist sect on the death of Calvin in 1564, he does not appear as villain in the works of Artus Désiré until the publication of the *Singerie des Huguenots*, etc. in 1573.

The conclusion is clear. In all periods of social upheaval there are individuals who remain so totally wedded to the past, or to what they conceive to be the past, that they are relatively untouched by current controversies between more progressive groups groping towards a more viable future. Artus Désiré leaves the impression of such a man, an accurate observer, perhaps, of day-to-day occurrences, but utterly incapable of comprehending the larger sweep of events. He was an *attardé* in the full sense of the word.

From the literary standpoint the works of Artus Désiré present almost no interest. The oblivion into which he fell almost as soon as he ceased writing was well deserved, and it is not our purpose here to revive him as a serious literary figure. His style is uniformly flat and prosaic; his lines are filled with padding to satisfy his rhythmic requirements; his themes are repetitive and scarcely "poetic" in the usual sense; his humor when he attempts it is heavy; and his satire is more often vituperative than barbed. The few bright spots are those in which he stigmatizes the human foibles of his contemporaries in occasionally earthy terms, as in describing the pretentiousness of the "femmes théologiennes," in detailing the tricks of the "taverniers," or in listing the current blasphemies, to which he objected as mortal sins, but of which he became the unwitting cataloguer.

Nor does any particular interest attach to his theological views. His system is that of the Catholic Church in its most fundamental orthodoxy. He defends repeatedly all the positions challenged by the Protestants: the mass and sacrament of the altar; the obedience owed to the clergy, despite their shortcomings, from the pope to the parish priest; respect for the church fathers; confession and fasting; the necessity of "good works" to achieve salvation. But his defense is for the most part weak and unimaginative: he relies heavily on authority and tradition, and resorts constantly to abusive language to "prove" his points. It is doubtful if many of those who had begun to question the religion of their fathers were persuaded by Désiré's arguments to return to orthodoxy.

In general his social analysis is of no greater interest than his theology, from which his social views derive. But there are at least three points which should be stressed. He paints a picture of conditions within the church and among the clergy that are horrifying. Coming from Protestant sources such testimony as he gives of pride, venality, indifference, corruption, wordliness, and carnal indulgence would be subject to caution. From him it must be accepted as true, if not understated.

Nor is there any reason not to believe him when he asserts that these abuses within the church are a primary cause of defections to protestantism. His estimate of the number of defectors varied. While on one occasion he assured the king that he had the support of his gendarmerie by one hundred to one, his usual estimate of the rate of defection ranged between "les trois pars" (Secret Conseil) and "les quatre pars" (Grands jours du parlement de Dieu). It is not possible to guess the actual number, especially since, before the outbreak of civil war many people had probably made no clear decision, and while unsympathetic to the plight of the church, had not broken with it.

A third most revealing side of his work is the violence of his attacks on the Protestants. Désiré never mentioned in his published works the massacre of Saint Barthélémy. But after August 1572 he called as persistently for just such a slaughter as he had before the event. It was as though, in his opinion, the results of the massacre were so inadequate that it might just as well not have taken place at all. In every one of his major works between 1547 and 1578 he appealed to the civil authorities to exterminate every heretic and even those (like Michel de l'Hospital, whom he singled out for special condemnation in the Secret Conseil) who showed any tendency to come to terms with the dissident sect.

Some slight additional interest is attached to his career for the role he played in several literary, or merely propaganda controversies involving more important figures than himself, for example his efforts to discredit Marot's translations of the psalms. And he was a central figure in the campaign against Geneva between 1556 and 1560, a campaign which pitted him against

Calvin and de Bèze, as well as other less known defenders of the new faith.

By their nature his activities should have secured him powerful backers among church leaders in France; and he does appear to have had some connections with the Sorbonne as well as in the Parlement of Paris. Although his *Contrepoison* was officially repudiated by the Sorbonne when challenged by Monluc, bishop of Valence, it continued to appear thereafter with the approval of the Sorbonne; and there is no other evidence that his opinions and recommendations were unacceptable to the church. But he does not appear to have profited much personally from these relations in the hierarchy; in fact, his persistent criticism of the corruption that was current in appointing to benefices must have been an embarrassment to more urbane spokesmen for the orthodox position, men like the cardinal de Lorraine and Ronsard, who were themselves among the principal beneficiaries of the corrupt system he decried.

The true role of Artus Désiré in 16th century France is thus clear. Incapable of any subtlety in evaluating the causes of division in the nation, and unable by his eloquence to persuade stray souls to return to the fold of the Catholic church, he nevertheless had a humble part to play. By ceaseless repetition of his dogmatic truths in the enormous mass of his published works, he may have dissuaded some from abandoning the religion of their fathers; and by his constant appeals for violence in coping with the new religion, he undoubtedly helped create the atmosphere in which a violent solution to the problem was finally attempted. He must bear his share of responsibility for the Saint Barthélemy massacre, and for the religious and political intransigeance of his lineal descendants in the League.

NORTH CAROLINA STUDIES IN THE ROMANCE LANGUAGES AND LITERATURES

I.S.B.N. Prefix 0-88438

Recent Titles

JACQUES DE LA TAILLE'S. "LA MANIERE," A CRITICAL EDITION, by Pierre Han. 1970. (No. 93). -893-X.

THE MAJOR THEMES OF EXISTENTIALISM IN THE WORK OF JOSÉ ORTEGA Y GASSET, by Janet Winecoff Díaz. 1970. (No. 94). -894-8.

CHARLES NODIER: HIS LIFE AND WORKS, by Sarah Fore Bell. 1971. (No. 95). -895-6.

RACINE AND SENECA, by Ronald W. Tobin. 1971. (No. 96). -896-4.

LOPE DE VEGA "EL PEREGRINO EN SU PATRIA," edición de Myron A. Peyton. 1971. (No. 97). -897-2.

CRITICAL REACTIONS AND THE CHRISTIAN ELEMENT IN THE POETRY OF PIERRE DE RONSARD, by Mark S. Whitney. 1971. (No. 98). -898-0.

THE REV. JOHN BOWLE. THE GENESIS OF CERVANTEAN CRITICISM, by Ralph Merritt Cox. 1971. (No. 99). -899-9.

THE FOUR INTERPOLATED STORIES IN THE "ROMAN COMIQUE": THEIR SOURCES AND UNIFYING FUNCTION, by Frederick Alfred De Armas. 1971. (No. 100). -900-6.

LE CHASTOIEMENT D'UN PERE A SON FILS, A CRITICAL EDITION, edited by Edward D. Montgomery, Jr. 1971. (No. 101). -901-4.

LE ROMMANT DE "GUY DE WARWIK" ET DE "HEROLT D'ARDENNE," edited by D. J. Conlon. 1971. (No. 102). -902-2.

THE OLD PORTUGUESE "VIDA DE SAM BERNARDO," EDITED FROM ALCOBAÇA MANUSCRIPT ccxci/200, WITH INTRODUCTION, LINGUISTIC STUDY, NOTES, TABLE OF PROPER NAMES, AND GLOSSARY, by Lawrence A. Sharpe. 1971. (No. 103). -903-0.

A CRITICAL AND ANNOTATED EDITION OF LOPE DE VEGA'S "LAS ALMENAS DE TORO," by Thomas E. Case. 1971. (No. 104). -904-9.

LOPE DE VEGA'S "LO QUE PASA EN UNA TARDE," A CRITICAL, ANNOTATED EDITION OF THE AUTOGRAPH MANUSCRIPT, by Richard Angelo Picerno. 1971. (No. 105). -905-7.

OBJECTIVE METHODS FOR TESTING AUTHENTICITY AND THE STUDY OF TEN DOUBTFUL "COMEDIAS" ATTRIBUTED TO LOPE DE VEGA, by Fred M. Clark. 1971. (No. 106). -906-5.

THE ITALIAN VERB. A MORPHOLOGICAL STUDY, by Frede Jensen. 1971. (No. 107). -907-3.

A CRITICAL EDITION OF THE OLD PROVENÇAL EPIC "DAUREL ET BETON," WITH NOTES AND PROLEGOMENA, by Arthur S. Kimmel. 1971. (No. 108). -908-1.

FRANCISCO RODRIGUES LOBO: DIALOGUE AND COURTLY LORE IN RENAISSANCE PORTUGAL, by Richard A. Preto-Rodas. 1971. (No. 109). -909-X.

RAIMOND VIDAL: POETRY AND PROSE, edited by W. H. W. Field. 1971. (No. 110). -910-3.

RELIGIOUS ELEMENTS IN THE SECULAR LYRICS OF THE TROUBADOURS, by Raymond Gay-Crosier. 1971. (No. 111). -911-1.

THE SIGNIFICANCE OF DIDEROT'S "ESSAI SUR LE MERITE ET LA VERTU," by Gordon B. Walters. 1971. (No. 112). -912-X.

PROPER NAMES IN THE LYRICS OF THE TROUBADOURS, by Frank M. Chambers. 1971. (No. 113). -913-8.

STUDIES IN HONOR OF MARIO A. PEI, edited by John Fisher and Paul A. Gaeng. 1971. (No. 114). -914-6.

DON MANUEL CAÑETE, CRONISTA LITERARIO DEL ROMANTICISMO Y DEL POSROMANTICISMO EN ESPAÑA, por Donald Allen Randolph. 1972. (No. 115). -915-4.

Recent Titles

THE TEACHINGS OF SAINT LOUIS. A CRITICAL TEXT, by David O'Connell. 1972. (No. 116). *-916-2.*

HIGHER, HIDDEN ORDER: DESIGN AND MEANING IN THE ODES OF MALHERBE, by David Lee Rubin. 1972. (No. 117). *-917-0.*

JEAN DE LE MOTE "LE PARFAIT DU PAON," édition critique par Richard J. Carey. 1972. (No. 118). *-918-9.*

CAMUS' HELLENIC SOURCES, by Paul Archambault. 1972. (No. 119). *-919-7.*

FROM VULGAR LATIN TO OLD PROVENÇAL, by Frede Jensen. 1972. (No. 120). *-920-0.*

GOLDEN AGE DRAMA IN SPAIN: GENERAL CONSIDERATION AND UNUSUAL FEATURES, by Sturgis E. Leavitt. 1972. (No. 121). *-921-9.*

THE LEGEND OF THE "SIETE INFANTES DE LARA" (*Refundición toledana de la crónica de 1344* versión), study and edition by Thomas A. Lathrop. 1972. (No. 122). *-922-7.*

STRUCTURE AND IDEOLOGY IN BOIARDO'S "ORLANDO INNAMORATO," by Andrea di Tommaso. 1972. (No. 123). *-923-5.*

STUDIES IN HONOR OF ALFRED G. ENGSTROM, edited by Robert T. Cargo and Emanuel J. Mickel, Jr. 1972. (No. 124). *-924-3.*

A CRITICAL EDITION WITH INTRODUCTION AND NOTES OF GIL VICENTE'S "FLORESTA DE ENGANOS," by Constantine Christopher Stathatos. 1972. (No. 125). *-925-1.*

LI ROMANS DE WITASSE LE MOINE. *Roman du treizième siècle.* Édité d'après le manuscrit, fonds français 1553, de la Bibliothèque Nationale, Paris, par Denis Joseph Conlon. 1972. (No. 126). *-926-X.*

EL CRONISTA PEDRO DE ESCAVIAS. *Una vida del Siglo XV*, por Juan Bautista Avalle-Arce. 1972. (No. 127). *-927-8.*

AN EDITION OF THE FIRST ITALIAN TRANSLATION OF THE "CELESTINA," by Kathleen V. Kish. 1973. (No. 128). *-928-6.*

MOLIÈRE MOCKED. THREE CONTEMPORARY HOSTILE COMEDIES: *Zélinde, Le portrait du peintre, Élomire Hypocondre*, by Frederick Wright Vogler. 1973. (No. 129). *-929-4.*

C.-A. SAINTE-BEUVE. *Chateaubriand et son groupe littéraire sous l'empire.* Index alphabétique et analytique établi par Lorin A. Uffenbeck. 1973. (No. 130). *-930-8.*

THE ORIGINS OF THE BAROQUE CONCEPT OF "PEREGRINATIO," by Juergen Hahn. 1973. (No. 131). *-931-6.*

THE "AUTO SACRAMENTAL" AND THE PARABLE IN SPANISH GOLDEN AGE LITERATURE, by Donald Thaddeus Dietz. 1973. (No. 132). *-932-4.*

FRANCISCO DE OSUNA AND THE SPIRIT OF THE LETTER, by Laura Calvert. 1973. (No. 133). *-933-2.*

ITINERARIO DI AMORE: DIALETTICA DI AMORE E MORTE NELLA Vita Nuova, by Margherita De Bonfils Templer. 1973. (No. 134). *-934-0.*

L'IMAGINATION POÉTIQUE CHEZ DU BARTAS, by Bruno Braunrot. 1973. (No. 135). *-935-9.*

Symposia

LOS NARRADORES HISPANOAMERICANOS DE HOY, edited by Juan Bautista Avalle-Arce. 1973. (No. 1). *-951-0.*

When ordering please cite the *ISBN Prefix* plus the last four digits for each title.

Send orders to:
International Scholarly Book Service, Inc.
P.O. Box 4347
Portland, Oregon 97208
U.S.A.

www.ingramcontent.com/pod-product-compliance
Lightning Source LLC
Chambersburg PA
CBHW030236240426
43663CB00037B/1173